DEADLY CANADIAN WOMEN

The Stories Behind the Crimes of Canada's Most Notorious Women

DEADLY CANADIAN WOMEN

The Stories Behind the Crimes of Canada's Most Notorious Women

QUAGMIRE
PRESS

The Publisher: Quagmire Press Ltd.
Website: www.quagmirepress.com

Library and Archives Canada Cataloguing in Publication

MacQuarrie, Patricia, 1976–
    Deadly Canadian Women: The Stories Behind the Crimes of Canada's
Most Notorious Women/ Patricia MacQuarrie.

Includes bibliographical references.
ISBN 978-0-9783409-2-6

    1. Women murderers—Canada. 2. Murder—Canada. I. Title.

HV6517.M33 2008   364.152'30820971   C2007-906364-0

Project Director: Lisa Wojna
Project Editor: Nicholle Carrière
Production: Vicky Tricket
Cover Design: Joy Dirto
Cover Image: Photos.com

PC: P5

Contents

~

Dedication

I would like to dedicate this book to two men. First, my dad, who was an amazing man and will be missed forever. Dad, you gave me spirit and stubbornness, ambition and dedication. I hope I make you proud.

Second, to my handsome husband, who gives me unconditional love and support and puts up with my stubbornness and "writer's moods." I will love you forever.

~

Acknowledgements

This book would not have been possible without the work of the following individuals: Brian Vallée for his works *The Torso Murder: The Untold Story of Evelyn Dick* and *Life With Billy*; Stephan Williams for *Invisible Darkness*; Rudy Weibe and Yvonne Johnson for *Stolen Life: The Journey of a Cree Woman*; Lisa Priest for her compendium *Women Who Killed*; and David Bagby for *Dance with the Devil: A Memoir of Murder and Loss*. Thank you to all the newspaper journalists and writers who document Canada's history on a daily basis. Without them, this project would never have been started.

I would also like to thank my Mum, who has always been a writer and a role model, and Lisa, for her guidance and loquaciousness. Thank you to my family for their extended support and my editor, Nicholle, for her hard work on this project.

My husband has always given me his support and holds a true belief in me, even when my own starts to waver. Thank you for everything that you are.

~

Introduction

Murder. Homicide. First-degree, second-degree. Infanticide, manslaughter. They all mean the same thing. Someone died. Someone else killed them. What follows are the stories of women who, by some method, for some reason, made the decision to end the life of another person. Many are "normal" women who, having reached a certain point, made a deadly decision. Others are from the edges of society, the forgotten ones, women at whom we can point a finger and say, "Oh, I see why she did it." But the truth is that all the stories in this book, all the lives these women lived, were lived by another before. But, unlike these women, those who came before did not always choose to kill.

Some of the women in this book have impacted the Canadian criminal justice system immensely. Karla Homolka became a lightning rod for the unfairness of plea bargains and redefined the way the average Canadian viewed a woman's role in murder. Shirley Turner sparked investigations that led to major changes in the child welfare system in Newfoundland. Jane Stafford's case led courts to accept being a battered wife as a defence. Deana Emard and Jamie Gladue helped to define the application of Section 718.2(e) of the Criminal Code when sentencing aboriginal offenders. Every one of these women caused a media storm, partly because of the fact that each was a woman.

My goal is to tell the story of these murderers, to give the details of their lives that led up to their crimes. At points, the content may be graphic. This is not simply for entertainment, and I do not want to revictimize the families of those affected. My aim is to show the monstrosity of the crimes.

～

Chapter One

Teresa Senner

In the centre of British Columbia, nestled in the Nechako Valley, lies the quaint town of Vanderhoof. Situated alongside the Nechako River with the rolling mountains as silent sentries in the distance, the 5000 people of Vanderhoof live a peaceful, relaxed life. It's a place where kids play outside after dark, folks look out for one another and the lines between family and neighbour blur. The people who live here are strong and resilient, like the wild forests and unyielding mountains that surround them, and it's the land that provides fuel for the thriving agriculture and forestry industries, which are the backbone of the area's economy. Like many a small town, it's a place where, at times, you simply can't survive without the support of your neighbours.

If the 17 churches in town are any indication, the people of Vanderhoof are a faithful lot with strong Christian values and a deep sense of community. When the Nechako River swells, as it often does, hundreds gather to lay sand bags to protect the homes of their fellow citizens. And when one of their own is in trouble, they rally.

Among the banks and government offices, the museums and historical parks, are the Nechako School District offices. Comprised of two floors of friendly employees, these busy offices set the backdrop for the most notorious love triangle and murder in the area's history. What follows is a story that gripped the minds of area residents and called them to action like few other situations ever had before. ∞

O ne of the school district's human resources clerks in 1998 was Teresa Senner. She was born in Oregon in 1962, and though her family immigrated to Canada when Senner was two years old, she never applied for citizenship. Regardless, the small community and district co-workers embraced her. Unfortunately, for all her warmth and humour, Teresa was not lucky in love. She married early in life and had two sons. When the marriage eventually ended, she met Guy Raymond, and she and her sons moved in with him. She was happy for a while, but Norman Wicks, the charismatic principal of W.L. MacLeod Elementary School, soon turned her head.

Wicks was a popular principal at both Mapes and W.L Macleod elementary schools. He danced in the hallways and always had pockets full of jellybeans for eager students. He disciplined, not with authority, but with true affection for the children. Pupils who were sent to the office for disciplinary action would instead get candy from the principal. He often roared up to the school on his Harley-Davidson motorcycle. Co-workers described him as their own personal cheerleader. He took it upon himself to do things like flood the ice rink at Mapes school or buy students Krazy Karpets in the winter. He was well known in the area for his friendly, outgoing personality. His job often took him to the Nechako School District offices for administrative meetings. It was there that Teresa met Norman Wicks.

An avid weightlifter and woodcutter, Wicks had a toned physique. He was considered attractive both inside and out by people in the district. His common-law wife, Joyce Upex, was also a principal in the district. The two were an administrative power couple. Yet one day Norman sashayed right up to Teresa's desk and into her heart. The pair started meeting secretly in 1998, as neither wanted their common-law spouses to know of the relationship. As it turned out, they were pretty good at hiding their affair. No one at the close-knit office knew about it, even though it continued for years.

As it goes in small towns and in faithless unions, Joyce began to suspect her partner of indiscretions in 2001. She confronted him, telling him she knew about his interoffice romance. But she wasn't suspicious of Senner. She was convinced that Norman was having an affair with the district superintendent's secretary, Cheryl Pershall. Wicks would not admit to a thing. Joyce confronted Cheryl, but she also denied the relationship. Teresa Senner's name never came up in any of Cheryl's discussions with either Pershall or Wicks. Whether her suspicions ran too deep or the call of a better job was too strong is not known, but in September 2001, Joyce packed her bags and took a leave of absence from her role as principal in Vanderhoof and headed to White Rock, near Vancouver. Although she had left Norman behind physically, the couple maintained a long-distance relationship that relied heavily on telephone calls and email. Norman, however, told Teresa a different story. She was under the distinct impression that he was now a free man, ready to give himself over entirely to her.

In 2002, Norman moved to a new home outside of town. Senner and Wicks now had more freedom to enjoy each other's company away from the prying eyes of the townsfolk. Teresa was still living with her common-law spouse, so she and Norman had to continue being secretive. One day, when Teresa was visiting, Cheryl Pershall arrived on Wicks' doorstep. She couldn't help but notice her co-worker's car in the driveway, since Cheryl and Teresa knew each other from work. But up to that point, neither knew just how much they had in common. Pershall put it all together when Wicks answered the door buck-naked. Norman denied it at first, but eventually admitted his long-time affair with both Teresa and Cheryl. Although nonplussed, Pershall got over the indiscretion and continued her relationship with Wicks, which had begun five years earlier. Somehow, through all this, Teresa remained clueless.

Tension between Teresa and Norman began to ripen by late 2002. She wanted him to commit to her in a formal and legal way. He argued that marriage would happen further down the line. The two had battles over the issue, but the deeper problems remained unrecognized, or at least unacknowledged by Senner.

For Wicks, November 20, 2002, started like any other day. It was business as usual at work, and Norman walked down the hall with his students, attended meetings and probably flirted with a few women. As per usual, and despite the fact that he was at work, Wicks spent time throughout the day emailing Teresa. But she was not her usual warm, fun-loving self. She was furious with him. Her frustrations appeared to stem from a housewarming party that co-workers were throwing for him that upcoming weekend. Norman's usual discretion failed him, and he let it slip that Joyce was invited to the housewarming. Teresa began questioning if Wicks had truly ended his relationship with Upex. When she learned that Joyce was actually planning to attend the party, Teresa became enraged. It is clear that she finally recognized that Norman Wicks was not a one-woman man. In an email Senner sent Wicks through the school district's email network, she wrote, "Well this is truly the last f***ing straw." Senner then switched from the district's email system and logged onto her private email account. From that account, she wrote, "You have played me for a fool, but just stand back now and watch what I am f***ing capable of and know that you have brought it on yourself with your f***ing lies. I hate you more than I ever knew I was capable of."

Within minutes of sending that last email, Teresa left her office for the day. She drove to the parking lot of W.L. MacLeod Elementary. At 3:30 PM, she was seen sitting in her car, but she never entered the school. She then drove to Wicks' new home on Vines Road, about 15 minutes away.

Teresa was vicious when she arrived. She kicked in the back door and stormed into the house. She phoned Norman's cellphone from his home phone and left a message. From there, she went straight to his computer and turned it on. She connected to his email and started reading. Shock set in. Her suspicions about the ongoing relationship between Upex and Wicks were confirmed, but Senner discovered there were other women in Wicks' life as well. She immediately tried his cellphone again, and when that failed, phoned Norman at the school. Using the old "It's an emergency" ruse, Teresa had him summoned from an afternoon meeting. He spoke on the phone for a few minutes, and when he returned to the meeting, he appeared distraught and unfocused. He quickly wrapped the meeting up and left the school.

For the next 23 minutes after presumably yelling at Wicks, Senner read emails to and from Cheryl Pershall that left no doubt as to the state of that relationship, as well as ongoing correspondence with two other women that Norman was courting. He had a lady on the go in the Okanagan and another in the United States. It was all too much for Teresa, who decided to face her troubles head on. She sent bitter and angry emails to each woman, leaving no doubt about her relationship with Wicks. Meanwhile, as Norman was heading home, he picked up the angry messages that Teresa had left on his voice mail. He attempted to call her at his house, but she wouldn't answer the phone. When Teresa heard Norman pull into the driveway, she apparently shut down the computer and raced downstairs for a fight. That altercation ended quickly, but not quietly.

However, according to Senner's testimony, Wicks came in while she was still on the computer. They began arguing and "things started flying." Lamps were knocked off tables, and the TV was overturned. Teresa later stated that she tried to leave the house, but Norman grabbed her wrists and insisted that she stay. They ended up in the kitchen, where there was a knife lying on the counter. She explained that because she didn't want anyone to get hurt, she picked up the knife. In her testimony during her second-degree murder trial, she stated:

> "Norm said, 'Oh, my God,' and he let go of my right hand, and I thought, 'What's the deal,' because the knife was pointed towards me. I pointed it towards me, so it couldn't have hurt Norm. I think he thought I was going to hurt myself, because he twisted it [my hand] back to take the knife, and then I let go, and he started to step back, and he said, 'You stabbed me!' And I said, 'I did not. That's ridiculous.'"

Teresa went on to testify that Norman stumbled backwards and fell down the stairs, but that she didn't realize it right away. She also didn't realize that the knife had sliced 15 centimetres into Wicks' groin. Teresa said that once Norman had fallen, she immediately began cleaning up the mess their violent fight had caused both in the kitchen and the computer room. Only after going back to where he lay did she see any blood. She testified that she then drove to a neighbour's home and called the police, the ambulance and Raymond, her common-law spouse. She then returned to the house, where she picked up the knife, walked down to the river behind Wicks' house and threw the knife into the water. By the time the police arrived, only an hour after Norman had left the school, his body was cold to the touch.

The small town was shocked to hear that the beloved principal had been murdered. Co-workers were even more shocked when police arrested Teresa Senner. After a long wait, the case went to trial at the end of April 2005. The courthouse was packed. Senner's sons attended the trial virtually every day, as did many of her supporters. The town came together and, in all, 50 people presented letters to the court stating what a kind and generous person Teresa was and that she was a valuable and contributing member of their community. The media covered the case extensively, especially after Wicks' "love hexagon" came to light.

On May 19, 2005, the jury decided that Senner was guilty of manslaughter rather than second-degree murder. They obviously thought that she had killed Wicks in a fit of jealous rage.

Teresa's testimony had been dramatic, but Judge Glen Parrett didn't buy it. During his sentencing decision, he stated that he simply did not believe that she had time to do all she said she had done in the eight minutes from the computer being turned off to calling the police. He found it inconceivable that during a fight so filled with rage, when Senner had just learned of all Wicks' indiscretions, she could calmly clean up the mess the fight had made and not realize that her long-term lover lay dying in a pool of blood at the bottom of the stairs.

According to Judge Parrett, Teresa heard Norman come home, turned off the computer and ran down to meet him. A fight ensued that was fast and violent. Senner plunged a knife into Wicks' leg, severing his femoral artery. He fell down the stairs and was left to bleed to death. Senner then picked up the weapon, walked down to the river and threw it in, and finally called the police. She then got back in her car and drove home to her partner because, she later stated to police, she felt that she needed to explain to him that "something was coming."

Although the Crown asked that Teresa be remanded to prison, Judge Parrett decided to sentence her to two years less a day, the sentence to be served in the community. She was given a curfew of 8:00 PM and had to meet with an officer of the court regularly. She was not allowed to leave the Vanderhoof area without informing the police and the court, she had to abstain from owning any firearms for 10 years and submit her DNA to the RCMP DNA database, but she was basically free. In closing, Judge Parrett also recommended that Teresa attend counselling to help her with her "intellectualizing" of the crime. He chastised Teresa for not taking responsibility for her actions during her testimony because she had repeatedly used comments such as "stuff just started flying," rather than accepting her part in the chaos. He pointed out that Teresa had also called the whole affair "unfortunate" but never apologized or accepted responsibility for the killing of Norman Wicks. But the 50 letters of support played heavily in his decision, and Judge Parrett stated that the people of the town had effectively shown what a contributing member of society Teresa was.

The conditional sentence caused outrage in Western Canada, and the newspapers immediately jumped on Judge Parrett for his sentence. Headlines such as "Crimes of Passion are Still Crimes," "Flawed Justice" and "No Jail Time for Philanderer's Jealous Killer" started showing up in both local and regional newspapers. Many columnists across the country felt that Teresa had received leniency because she was a woman. Others felt that it was the justice system as a whole that had failed by not placing Teresa in jail. In his defence, Judge Parrett explained that the stabbing resulted from an uncommon and uncharacteristic rage and that Teresa was unlikely to stab another lover to death.

Nechako Valley MP Jay Hill spoke about Senner's sentencing during a House of Commons session, berating the court for its leniency. He spoke to the fact that she had received such a mild sentence and questioned whether a man would have received similar treatment. But in the end, the Crown did not appeal the sentence. And although Senner received almost unprecedented support, as far as murderesses go, the people of Vanderhoof were split in their loyalties. In such a small town, everyone seemed to have an opinion about her sentence. Some believed that Teresa should have gone to jail, while others felt the shock of learning about her lover's many other liaisons was enough to justify a sudden rage. Many also felt that had she truly wanted to kill Wicks, she would have stabbed him somewhere other than his upper thigh. Some felt she didn't have the right to be upset at Wicks' indiscretions, considering she was one of them, and others sympathized with her, feeling she had gotten caught up in a horrible situation. Presumably, these differences in opinion will never be resolved.

In August 2007, Teresa Senner completed her conditional sentence and is now a free woman. She no longer lives in the Vanderhoof area.

~

Chapter Two

Shirley Turner

Dr. Andrew Bagby was a new and well-liked family practice resi-
dent in the small community of Latrobe, Pennsylvania. He arrived
at work late and uncharacteristically agitated on November 5,
2001. Shirley Turner, his ex-girlfriend, had shown up on his door-
step at 5:30 that morning. This was especially surprising, since he
had just broken up with her. In addition, two days before, he had
put her on a plane back to Iowa. When he left for work, he reluc-
tantly agreed to meet with Shirley later in the day. He assured his
supervisor, Dr. Clark Simpson, that the meeting would not inter-
fere with the dinner plans they had for 7:30 that night. He was
wrong. Not only did Andrew not show up for dinner, he didn't come
to work the next morning. When Andrew Bagby's bullet-ridden
body was discovered in a local park, attention quickly turned to his
recent ex, Shirley Turner. Although a case was rapidly built against
her, it never went to trial. Before the final curtain closed on the
story, another Bagby was dead. ❧

TROUBLE FROM THE START

Shirley Turner was born in Kansas in 1961. Her father was an American serviceman who met her mother while he was stationed in Newfoundland. He brought his new bride back to the States when he returned home. The marriage was short but produced four children. After Turner's parents separated, her mother returned to Newfoundland with the children. Because Shirley had an American father and a Canadian mother, she held both American and Canadian citizenship, a fact that would play an important role in her life some 40 years later.

Shirley was raised in the tiny fishing village of Daniel's Harbour in Newfoundland from the age of seven. Her family was poor and moved frequently. Friends recall Shirley being jealous of anyone who lived in better circumstances. Shirley entered the undergraduate program at Sir Wilfred Grenfell College in Corner Brook, Newfoundland, in 1980. She majored in chemistry, with the intention of eventually becoming a doctor. However, her life circumstances caused her to take a much longer road than she had originally intended.

She married in 1981 and, even though she had not finished her first degree and did not have a teaching certificate, took a job as a teacher. For the next 10 years, Shirley alternated between finishing her degree, having children and teaching. She divorced her first husband in 1988 and married her high school sweetheart. They separated in 1991 and divorced six years later.

In all, Shirley had three children, but for most of their lives, the children did not live with her. The paternal grandmother of her two oldest children played a major role in their lives, and they often stayed with her while Shirley was either working or attending university away from the small town of Daniel's Harbour. The father of the youngest child retained custody of her, though according to the terms of the divorce, Shirley was to have full custody. Turner finished her undergraduate degree in 1994 and almost immediately decided to attend med school.

Most who knew her would say that Shirley could talk her way out of anything. She was friendly, lively and personable. She loved to tell stories and talked, almost nonstop at times, to anyone who would listen. Her outgoing, persuasive personality often got her out of situations that could paralyze most other people. Intelligent, accomplished individuals recall being swayed by her, only to shake their heads at themselves later.

The first documented sign of serious trouble in Shirley Turner's life was a report of child abuse made against her by a boarder she took on in St. John's late in 1993. He claimed that Turner was physically and emotionally abusive towards her children. He saw her slap the children and be downright nasty to them verbally. The Department of Social Services met with the children in the presence of their school principal, and they didn't dispute the claims. They told the social worker that their mother spanked them with an open hand and occasionally a belt. The social worker tried to contact Shirley and left messages for her at her apartment, but she never returned the phone calls. For some reason, the Department of Social Services closed the file on the allegations of abuse without establishing contact with Turner at all.

Directly following the long-delayed completion of her undergraduate degree, Shirley was accepted into the Faculty of Medicine at Memorial University in St. John's, Newfoundland. She again left her children with relatives and completed her first year of studies. The children came to live with her for her second year and part of her third, and then they returned to relatives until she graduated as an MD in 1998. She complained that raising children was too difficult while trying to become a doctor. She completed her internships and residencies at various hospitals in Newfoundland, finally completing her studies in 2000.

According to her supervisors, during her time as a resident at a family practice clinic in St. John's, Dr. Turner was difficult to work with. She started off on the wrong foot by showing up two days late. She then promptly submitted the days she was available to work to her supervisors. Shirley frequently missed work and would offer unbelievable excuses, if she offered any at all. Once she even told supervisors that she had to stay home with her son, who was ill. It was a well-known fact among her peers at the time that her son lived in Daniel's Harbour and not with Shirley. When confronted with her lie by her supervisor, she changed her story, saying that she had been on the phone with him all night. Although her supervisor did not believe her, he could not prove otherwise.

Shirley was often defensive at work. She demanded that harsh or critical comments be removed from her evaluations. Physicians working with and supervising Shirley reported feeling manipulated by her and having their personal integrity attacked during disagreements. To protect themselves from her potentially damaging accusations, supervisors created a team approach to any confrontation or discussion of her work. It was the only time in 21 years of managing more than 400 residents that supervisors ever had to go to such extraordinary measures. So severe were the problems that Dr. Turner had to complete a most unusual remedial term at a family clinic in order to complete her residency requirements. Judging by future events, the question remains whether any of the disciplinary actions taken on her behalf were enough.

Shirley's personal life should also have triggered warning signs. While she was at university, she started dating a man nine years her junior. During the course of their relationship, he reported various assaults by Shirley, including one incident in which she attacked him with her shoes. Another time, she became so emotionally unstable that she was admitted to a Halifax hospital for an overnight psychiatric evaluation. She was treated, at least sporadically, on an outpatient basis by a psychiatrist for the next few years. The official relationship with the younger man was short-lived, but Shirley attempted to continue seeing him, almost to the point of stalking, for the next two years. Even when the man moved to a new city, and eventually new country, Shirley repeatedly called and showed up unannounced and uninvited at his home.

The final straw was when the man arrived home one evening to find a trail of blood leading to his apartment and Shirley propped up against his door. When he approached her, she slowly lifted her arm to hand him a piece of paper. It was a suicide note. Shirley had taken a mixture of antihistamines and sleep aids. The sleep aids were known to cause vomiting when taken in large doses. Being a doctor, Shirley would know this, and so it seems the intent of her performance was to affect the man rather than kill herself. She had also bashed her hands against the steps leading to the apartment in order to leave the blood trail. Even more revealing of her poor mental health was the message she left for her ex-lover the morning following this event—her voice poorly disguised, she informed him that she had died. After that incident, Shirley continued leaving messages for the man into early 2000. These were more disturbing and included direct threats on his life as well as harassing calls to his parents. As well, Shirley continued to visit him unannounced, even though she had begun a new relationship with an even younger man, Andrew Bagby. Years later, the man would fear for his life to the point where he would have friends sleep on his couch, and he kept a weapon near his bed in case Shirley turned up again. Her habit of harassing old boyfriends and showing up unannounced would repeat itself throughout Shirley's life.

A MEETING OF HEARTS?

Andrew Bagby was born in San Diego, California, on September 25, 1973. He grew up in Silicon Valley, a popular kid with a strong sense of humour and a gift for impersonating many different characters. Regarded as a best friend by quite a few people, he made friends easily wherever he went. Andrew excelled at school and completed a Bachelor of Science degree in biology from the University of California in 1995. He worked for a year at Stanford as a researcher while applying to medical schools all over North America. He was accepted into a small medical school in Newfoundland, which is what brought Andrew Bagby to Canada.

Andrew started his medical degree in 1996 at Memorial University. When he moved to St John's, he brought his fiancée, Heather, and she also enrolled at the university. The couple broke up during the summer following their first year, but remained close friends.

In 1999, Andrew was a third-year medical student, and Shirley Turner was a second-year resident. At this point, Shirley was still harassing her ex-boyfriend in Pennsylvania. Regardless, a relationship between Turner and Bagby developed, and the two spent a great deal of time together. Both agreed that the relationship was a casual one. Shirley said she had no intention of marrying Andrew because she already had two failed marriages and there was a substantial difference in their ages. Andrew made it clear to his parents that the relationship had no strings. Shirley was also usually friendly with Andrew's ex, Heather. But occasionally, she told Heather to stop trying to get Andrew back, even though Heather was in a new relationship.

Andrew received his MD in 2000, and at the end of that summer, Andrew and Shirley left Newfoundland together for jobs in different areas of the United States. Shirley, having finally completed her residency requirement, accepted a job in Sac City, Iowa. For agreeing to accept a permanent position as a doctor in their health-care clinics, the Trimark Physicians Corporation of Fort Dodge paid Shirley's moving expenses and gave her a large bonus in addition to her annual salary of around $171,000. Andrew wanted to become a surgeon, so he took a surgical residency in Syracuse, New York. Again, Shirley decided that the demands of child rearing were too much in addition to her day job, and she left her children in Canada. For the next year, Turner and Bagby maintained a long-distance relationship with infrequent visits.

Shirley, showing her disregard for responsibility, quit her position in Sac City, leaving a large financial debt with the clinic, and moved to an Alegent Health family practice clinic in Council Bluffs, Iowa, in the summer of 2001. Around the same time, Andrew decided against surgery and chose to move to a family practice residency program in Latrobe, Pennsylvania. Latrobe is a small town of about 9000, and he worked in an even smaller town named Saltsburg as part of his residency. He was well liked and, as is the way of small towns, started becoming known in the area. During the ensuing months, Shirley visited Andrew on occasion and stayed with him in his apartment.

The last time the two were together as a couple was a weeklong visit late in 2001 that Shirley made to Andrew's apartment. Andrew had planned to finally end the relationship during the visit. Although he had tried in the past, Shirley had refused to accept the separation. However, she agreed they could see other people during their long-distance relationship. During that visit, it came out that Andrew had started seeing a radiology clerk at the Latrobe hospital. The couple fought loudly about the other woman, but no violence took place. While Shirley was in town, the clerk received phone calls from an anonymous person who said that Andrew was seeing someone else. Andrew took Shirley to the airport on November 3, 2001, and, over lunch, ended their relationship. As soon as she got off the plane in Iowa, Shirley started her preparations for a drive back to Latrobe the following day.

MURDER ON THE RUN

On Sunday, November 4, 2001, Andrew was rudely awakened by the ringing of his phone. It was Shirley. Even though they had broken up the day before, she made Andrew promise to call her. He spoke to Shirley later that morning as promised and possibly that afternoon as well. At around 1:00 PM, unbeknownst to Andrew, Shirley loaded up her Rav4 and began the 15-hour drive to Latrobe.

Using cellphone records, police were able to get a clear picture of her travel. She called her supervisor at Alegent Health from Chicago, 740 kilometres from Council Bluffs, at around 8:00 PM on November 4, 2001. She told a staff member that she had a severe migraine and not to expect her at work the following day. It was supposed to be her first day of work. Then, 145 kilometres later, she made another phone call from South Bend, Indiana, just over halfway to Latrobe. Whom she called is not clear. At 5:30 AM on November 5, Shirley knocked on Andrew's door. She was aggressive and angry, attacking Andrew about ending their relationship. Andrew, insisting that he needed to leave, hesitantly agreed to meet with Shirley after work. He left her in his apartment.

When Bagby arrived at work, he told his supervisor, Dr. Simpson, about Turner's abrupt arrival. Knowing Shirley and her crazy antics, Simpson laughingly warned Bagby not to be late for the party at his house that night. Andrew assured his boss that the meeting would not last long.

From Andrew's apartment, Shirley again phoned in sick to work. Next she connected to the Internet and did some shopping. She also seems to have spent some time snooping around and discovered a box of condoms that Andrew had bought in preparation for his date with the radiology clerk. Is this what sent Shirley over the edge? It's hard to know. But she took the box and emptied its contents. The box ended up being a key piece of evidence against her just a few days later.

For Andrew, on the other hand, it was work as usual, including a trip to the Saltsburg clinic with his supervisor. The head nurse at the clinic saw Andrew leave just after 5:00 that evening. She is the last person known to have seen him alive besides his killer. His cellphone records show that he called Shirley's cellphone twice and then tried his own residence. What took place during those calls is not known, but at some point between 5:27 PM and 6:10 PM on November 5, Andrew arrived at Keystone State Park, about 11 kilometres from his home. Police believe Shirley met him there.

That evening, a man was walking home after a day of hunting. He noticed a Rav4 and a Toyota Corolla parked side by side in the day parking area of the park. He didn't see or hear anyone. Dr. Andrew Bagby was murdered near his car at some point after 6:10 PM. The hunter, returning for another day of hunting at 4:30 AM the next day, noticed that the Toyota Corolla was still there. The Rav4 was not.

If Shirley did kill Andrew as the police and many others believe, a timeline of her cellphone calls indicate his time of death. At 11:30 PM, she used her cellphone in her car. The car was three hours away in Cleveland, Ohio, so Shirley must have killed Andrew at around 8:30 PM on November 5, 2001. However, his body was not discovered until morning. As the sun rose, a Latrobe resident walking through the park at 6:00 AM saw the body. Overnight, the temperature had dropped enough the cover the body in frost, indicating that Bagby's death had occurred at least a few hours before. Andrew was still wearing his hospital uniform and his hospital identification on a lanyard around his neck. He had been shot five times: once in the head, face and chest, as well as twice in the buttocks. He had also been hit with a blunt object in the back of the head. In his pocket was a receipt for condoms dated a few days earlier. Near his body was an unspent round of CCI brand ammunition. Andrew Bagby was legally pronounced dead on November 6, 2001, though everyone involved in the investigation believe his death actually occurred the night before.

The call Shirley made at 11:30 PM was to a supervisor at Alegent Health. She told the nurse that she had a headache and had remained in bed all day. She expected to come to work the next day, though not in time for her 9:00 AM shift. Shirley then told the nurse that she was currently driving on an interstate because she could drive fast. She said that she loved to drive fast. A very strange call indeed for someone suffering from a migraine.

At 9:00 AM the next morning, a nurse from Alegent Health left a message on Shirley's cellphone to let her know that a patient was expecting to see her at 10:30 AM. Shirley returned the call about 20 minutes later while driving. At that time, she was about 145 kilometres away. She told the nurse that she hadn't slept all night and would not make it to the appointment. She also told the nurse that she had to clean her car at a carwash, go home and take a shower, and then change her clothes.

Next, Shirley called Andrew's mother, Kathleen, at work to ask if she had heard from Andrew lately. Kathleen told Shirley that she hadn't spoken to Andrew for two days. She asked Shirley when she had last spoken to Andrew. Shirley lied and said that she hadn't spoken to him in the last three days, not since they had left each other at the airport. Signing off with Andrew's mother, she mentioned that she needed to clean herself up before seeing her first patient. At 11:00 AM, Shirley finally showed up for work, hair wet from just having showered. She saw three patients that day in Iowa, but 1600 kilometres away, she was becoming a suspect in Andrew Bagby's murder.

Hot on Her Trail

Three weeks before Andrew's murder, Shirley bought herself an HP22 Phoenix Arms semi-automatic .22-calibre handgun. When she bought the gun, the seller told her that if she needed the gun for personal protection, she should buy a permit that allowed her to carry it with her. Shirley never applied for the permit.

The gun Shirley bought was not a good one. It often malfunctioned and ejected live rounds of ammunition when fired. During lessons at the Bullet Hole in nearby Omaha, Nebraska, Shirley's shooting instructor told her to try switching from American Eagle ammunition to CCI. It didn't help. The gun still dropped live rounds. The day before Shirley's weeklong visit to see Bagby, she had a lesson with the new ammunition.

The gun was still not working properly. She was supposed to go to the Bullet Hole on November 5, but did not show up—she was in Pennsylvania.

Early in their investigation, police learned about the gun that Turner had registered in Iowa. When Council Bluff police asked Shirley about the gun on November 6, she at first told them that she had last seen it at her lesson on October 25. When they asked her for it, she told them it was in her house but that she couldn't find it. Then she said it had been stolen from her car, though the carrier box for the gun was still there. She changed her story once more and told them she had given it to Bagby. She also told the police that she only owned American Eagle ammunition, but the police knew from an interview with her firearms instructor that she also owned CCI brand ammunition, the same type that killed Andrew, as well as the same calibre of weapon. Neither the murder weapon nor Shirley's gun was ever found.

On November 9, a search warrant was executed at Shirley's apartment. In the trash, police found an empty condom box, the same one that Shirley had discovered just days earlier in Andrew's apartment. The serial number on the box matched the number from a receipt found on Andrew's body. The box was a key piece of evidence during court proceedings against Shirley. In addition, the police collected a pair of boots and the lint trap from her dryer.

As for Shirley, she started making phone calls to relatives and acquaintances. Andrew's father recalls Shirley's propensity for talking on the phone in his book, *Dance with the Devil*. The Bagbys started screening their phone calls shortly after Shirley began dating Andrew because she would call them and talk incessantly, sometimes keeping them on the phone for over an hour. This addiction to telling stories, especially on the phone, led Shirley to contradict herself over and over in various conversations with friends and relatives in the coming months. Her words would be used as evidence during court proceedings. One of the first people she called was Bagby's ex-fiancée, Heather, under the guise of calling to inform her of Andrew's death.

During the bizarre conversation, Shirley revealed that she had a miscarriage in October, though this was unlikely, and that she had given Andrew her gun because he had asked to borrow it. She continued calling Heather day and night throughout November. She was always intent on informing the poor girl that her relationship with Andrew was strong right up until his death and even inundated Heather with graphic sexual details.

Shirley also contacted classmates from Memorial University. To one, she stated that she had seen Andrew on November 5 but denied giving him a gun. She told another person that she had given Andrew the gun on November 5, because he had asked for it for his own protection. As well, she said that the police had not taken the clothes she was wearing the night she last saw Andrew. This information was provided to the police, who then executed another search warrant and seized those clothes.

Abruptly, one week after Andrew's murder, Shirley boarded a flight to Toronto, leaving most of her possessions behind. She never returned to the United States again. The reasons Shirley gave for her hasty departure constantly changed. To Andrew's parents, she stated that she had left on the advice of her lawyer. To her daughter, she said she had left because she was afraid that whoever killed Andrew had seen her and would try to kill her, too. She also told various family, friends and law officials that she had left to be with her son who had been in a car accident. However, the accident did not occur until after she had left the United States. Whatever the true reason, Shirley remained in Toronto for a short time and then settled in St. John's, Newfoundland. She would live there for the next two and a half years.

On November 19, 2001, two weeks after Bagby's murder, Pennsylvania State Troopers requested that the Newfoundland Constabulary open a file on Shirley with the purpose of tracking her movements in that province. In fact, Shirley's constant phone calls and sporadic visits to Heather's apartment led Heather to file a complaint and request routine surveillance on her apartment for her own safety. Indeed, Andrew's ex-fiancée was one of the first to be informed that Shirley was pregnant, by Shirley herself, despite her earlier claims to have suffered a miscarriage. During surveillance, officers saw Shirley throwing away some garbage, which they seized. In it, among other things, they found an ultrasound of a fetus with the conception date of October 2001. Shirley Turner and Andrew Bagby were listed as the parents.

ARREST, INCARCERATION AND EXTRADITION

Pennsylvania State Trooper Kirk Nolan phoned the Newfoundland Constabulary on November 27, 2001, to discuss Shirley Turner. The state troopers had a warrant for Turner's arrest on charges of murder in the first degree and criminal homicide. If Turner did not voluntarily accompany him, under arrest, back to Pennsylvania, the United States would apply for an extradition order in Canada. Shirley did not choose to leave voluntarily. On December 12, extradition proceedings were started to have Turner brought from Newfoundland to Pennsylvania to stand trial for Andrew's murder, a charge that could carry the death penalty. However, the United States authorities agreed not to apply the death penalty in exchange for being allowed to proceed with the extradition hearing.

A judge decided that it was in the public's interest for Turner to be arrested and brought before the court. Once in court, Shirley asked for bail. Both counsels, that for Canada and the United States and counsel for Turner agreed that she be released on a $75,000 recognizance. Shirley's psychiatrist put up $65,000. In Canada, a recognizance is not paid up front. The only time the money is ever paid is if the accused violates any of the conditions of release. Shirley's conditions were that she was required to attend court, report to the Newfoundland Constabulary, reside in St. John's, surrender both her passports, have no weapons and have no contact with Andrew's family and seven other individuals, including Andrew's ex-fiancée.

On November 14, 2002, almost a year later, the Canadian Chief Justice of the Supreme Court found enough evidence to commit Shirley Turner for extradition. She was placed into custody in the Newfoundland and Labrador Correctional Centre for Women in Clarenville.

While incarcerated, Shirley again proved difficult. She frequently argued with other inmates. One afternoon, she had seven different complaints made against her by other prisoners. Another day, Shirley was placed in lockdown for two days because she got into a fight with another woman, something that staff at the centre report as being highly irregular. She threatened to stab at least one inmate with a fork. Most of the inmates at the centre were afraid of her. She spent most of her time under suicide watch because the centre's staff questioned her mental health. Psychiatrists who evaluated her placed her at a moderate risk level for suicide, but also indicated that she was possibly suffering from an adjustment disorder resulting from the "loss" of a close friend. In all, 1978 suicide-watch observations were made for Shirley in her time at the centre. Unfortunately, this information was never passed on to the Crown or to social aid workers in the community.

Shirley appealed the extradition decision while incarcerated and requested interim release pending a decision on that appeal. Although challenged by both the Canadian and United States counsels, the Court of Appeal granted Shirley's release on January 9, 2003. Shirley's lawyer submitted an appeal that she not be surrendered to the United States because of the circumstantial nature of the case, her lack of adequate financial resources to defend herself in the U.S., the length of time she would be forced to be away from her children, and because, as a doctor, if she were found innocent of the charges, she would be a valuable member of Canadian society. On June 9, 2003, the chief justice denied all appeals and ordered her surrendered to U.S. authorities. Turner appealed this ruling as well, and a court date of September 25, 2003, was set. That court date was never held.

BABY BOY BAGBY

Dr. Shirley Turner gave birth to a son, Zachary, on July 18, 2002, at the Health Sciences Centre in St. John's. However, the controversy surrounding him started much earlier.

Shirley first contacted Child, Youth and Family Services (CYFS) through a friend. The friend told CYFS workers that Shirley needed help to create a plan for the baby in case she was extradited. At the beginning of May 2002, a worker called her to discuss options. Throughout the following months, Shirley went back and forth on adoption, foster care and having a variety of friends and family look after Zachary in the event she was extradited or incarcerated. The only thing she remained stead-fast about was that she did not want Andrew's parents to get custody. She gave a variety of reasons for not granting custody to the Bagbys. She worried that they would harm her son. She thought they might be disrespectful towards her and take it out on Zachary because they believed she had killed Andrew. She also said she worried about them taking the baby to California or even England. She was angry with them for not believing that Andrew was the father. Shirley went as far as firing her law-yer, who tried to convince her that the Bagbys were being sup-portive of her and that she should consider giving them some access to their grandchild. She reported to the CYFS worker at various times that she thought the Bagbys had tapped her phone, that they were stalking her and even at one point indicated that Kathleen Bagby had threatened to kill her. She never produced any evidence to justify these fears.

The Bagbys, on the other hand, started proceedings at the end of May to get either full custody or liberal access to the baby they considered their grandchild. They travelled to Newfoundland to attend the extradition hearings, and while in Canada, retained a family law lawyer. Through their lawyer, they asked the Unified Family Court for custody. They felt the emotional stress of having a father murdered and a mother charged with the murder could be potentially harmful to the child. As well, they worried about the emotional well-being of both the mother and child with such an uncertain future. They made it clear that they considered themselves the grandparents and asked for a paternity test to prove that their son was the father. They also contacted CYFS in mid-June through their lawyer to indicate that they wanted custody of the baby when it was born, that they were willing to relocate from California to Newfoundland, and that whoever the father was, they still wanted custody.

When Zachary was born, the Bagbys came to the hospital with presents for Shirley and her new baby. She refused to see them. The next day, the Bagbys requested that a custody restraining order be placed on Shirley to restrict her movements and prevent her from fleeing. Because there would be a delay before the case could be heard in front of a judge, they also requested an interim custody restraining order. That request was granted, and an order was issued stating that Shirley was not allowed to leave St. John's.

On August 6, 2002, a meeting took place between the Bagbys and Shirley to discuss custody. After much debate, both parties agreed that the grandparents could see the child for one hour per week, with a review to be scheduled in September. For the privilege of spending time with their grandson, the Bagbys had to pay all costs associated with the visit, including Shirley and Zachary's transportation and a court-appointed supervisor to oversee the meeting.

The Bagbys were excited at every visit. They revelled in every smile and laugh from their grandson. They brought presents for Zachary as well as larger items, including a car seat.

They also supplied Shirley with diapers and other necessities when they met weekly. The Bagbys hated having to see their son's killer, but seeing Zachary made the visits worthwhile. He was their last connection to their son. In conversations with her caseworker, Shirley showed some softening in her attitude towards the Bagbys. When the review came up, the conditions were changed so that the Bagbys could see Zachary more often, this time at home, but they had to supply Shirley with a phone so they could reach her if necessary. These visits also went well according to Shirley, and she indicated to her caseworker in mid-November that if she were to be incarcerated following her upcoming extradition hearing, she would like to have the Bagbys appointed as Zachary's primary caregivers.

During this time, Shirley was also receiving counselling and support from a personal psychiatrist, Child, Youth and Family Services, and Community and Health Services. She had a health nurse visit her home every week for over a year, and she also had a parenting coach come to her home every day for over a month. As well, she took part in the Healthy Beginnings program to assist with child-rearing issues. The Newfoundland Government also provided financial assistance. They supplied her with bus passes, clothes for Shirley's older daughter, who was also residing with her, a crib for the courthouse along with a babysitter so that Zachary could come to the courthouse, as Shirley was still breastfeeding, and other incidentals.

On November 14, 2002, Shirley was ordered into custody to await extradition. The Bagbys picked Zachary up from his home, having been granted full guardianship for the duration of Shirley's incarceration. During that time, the Bagbys spent a lot of time and money ensuring that Shirley got to spend time with her son. Every week, they drove to Clarenville so that Shirley could have a two-day visit with Zachary. Typically, Shirley would get to visit with Zachary for a few hours in the morning and afternoon both days in a room at the centre. The Bagbys were required to be present for the visits, a fact that Shirley complained about bitterly.

When Shirley was granted bail in January 2003, she regained custody, and another consent order was prepared. This time, the Bagbys were given significantly more time with their grandson. The Bagbys had Zachary even more often because Shirley used them as babysitters whenever she wanted to go out. The result was what Shirley considered a developing friendship—the Bagbys considered it a necessary evil. In March, paternity results came back confirming that Andrew was Zachary's father.

In the summer of 2003, Shirley met a new man on one of her nights out at a bar in St. John's. They went on two dates, after which the man made it clear he did not want to see Shirley again. But Shirley was not interested in being rebuffed. Following the script from her past, she continued calling him and even told her friends that things were going well. In reality, he was

trying desperately to be rid of her. He called the police anonymously on a few occasions and told them that she was stalking
and harassing him, calling over 200 times in one month. She
often called him in the middle of the night and even claimed to
be pregnant by him. The man had the police call Turner's lawyer
to warn her to stop calling, but it didn't help. She never stopped
attempting to contact him.

A JUMP TO THE DEATH

On Saturday, August 16, 2003, the Bagbys spent a day at
the park with Shirley and Zachary. They went swimming and
ate some lunch. Everyone was happy, and the Bagbys did not
notice anything unusual about Shirley that day. They did
not know it would be the last time they would see their grandson alive.

The next day, Shirley went to the pharmacy and filled
a prescription for Ativan, a drug for anxiety containing benzo-
diazepine, which had been prescribed to her by her psychiatrist
in mid-July, a month earlier. That evening, Shirley's older son,
who was living with her at the time, said goodnight to her
around 11:00 PM. Shirley made a few phone calls to friends but
mostly was only able to leave voice messages. She left a message
for one friend that she was planning to stay the night at the
home of the man she had met in the bar. At around 11:30, her
son heard a car in the driveway. He realized it was his mother

leaving in her little Mercury Topaz and was surprised that she was taking Zachary with her so late at night.

Shirley drove out to an area called Kelligrews, about a half hour away, where the man she was pursuing lived. She pulled over to the side of the road at a location that allowed her to see the man's apartment and got stuck. Police believe she walked up to his car and placed two pictures on the ground— one of her and Zachary, one of her in lingerie. She also placed a used tampon on the ground. Was this an attempt to frame him for what she was about to do?

Next, Shirley returned to her car and gave her son a drink of milk. Police think she laced the milk with the Ativan tablets she had picked up earlier that day. The tablets would have made the child very sleepy but wouldn't kill him, a fact she would know as a doctor. Apparently, she then picked up Zachary, tied him to her using the sleeves of her jacket and walked out into the pouring rain.

Police believe she walked down an overgrown path to the coastal road and continued walking on the paths between Kelligrews and the Foxtrap area for about an hour and a half. At around 3:00 AM, a man monitoring the Foxtrap marina heard what he thought was a baby crying. When he went out to inspect, he saw the dark shape of a person moving away, but the person didn't respond to his calls.

At 6:30 in the morning on August 18, Shirley's oldest son woke up and found his mother gone. He called friends and family, but no one knew where she was, so he phoned the police to report her missing. Being that she was so well known in St. John's, the police began searching for her and her car right away. They phoned many of her friends, and from one, they learned about the message Shirley had left the previous night about staying with the man from the bar. When they contacted the man, he stated that Shirley had not spent the night with him. He explained that he hadn't seen her for quite a few days, but she was harassing him and his new girlfriend. When asked about the Mercury Topaz, the man said that he had seen a car like that near his home when he had gone to work that day. He had not known that Shirley even had a car and agreed to meet the police at the vehicle. It was later discovered that a neighbour of the man had also noticed the car. His wife told him to ignore it because she had often seen it parked there with a lady inside. Perhaps Shirley had often parked at that spot and watched the her ex-boyfriend's apartment.

When they searched the car, the police found Shirley's identification, her purse and Zachary's bottle and diaper bag. The bottle was half full, but officers dumped the contents out when they took it for evidence. It was never tested, so it will never be known for sure that Shirley gave Zachary Ativan using the bottle, but when toxicology tests were done on Zachary's body, he had extremely high levels of the drug in his system. The police also discovered the pictures Shirley had left, which led them to question the man further. He admitted that he was the anonymous caller the police had been in contact with regarding being harassed by Shirley.

That same day, an Ontario couple was out for a stroll along the beach with their dog. While walking near the Kelligrews, the husband saw something that looked like a body lying on the rocks. He told his wife to wait for the police at the start of the trail while he called 911. He did not see the baby lying a few feet up the beach. At 7:15 AM, when the call came in, the police descended on the beach. Shirley's body was dressed in platform heels and the clothing from the day before. Her jacket was found a few feet away with the arms still tied together. They found Zachary's body 50 metres farther up the beach.

After conducting autopsies on both bodies, the coroner ruled Shirley's death a suicide and Zachary's death a homicide. The Royal Newfoundland Constabulary also concluded that Shirley Turner had drowned both herself and her son, with no intervention by a third party. It seems that the end of the wharf at the Foxtrap marina is the most likely place for Shirley to have jumped into the ocean, holding her son in her arms while he was tied to her by her own jacket.

THE OFFICIAL INQUIRY

How was it that Shirley Turner was in direct contact with Community and Health Services, Child, Youth and Family Services, at least one psychiatrist and the Constabulary, and yet no one had foreseen that Zachary was in danger? Turner had multiple dealings with Child Welfare workers regarding her older children. She was on suicide watch almost the entire time she was incarcerated in the Newfoundland and Labrador Correctional Centre for Women, yet that information was never passed on to caseworkers in the community. Police had information regarding the harassment of one man, one of her former lovers had been murdered, and another was afraid for his life, yet no extra steps were taken to look into Turner's mental health.

What went wrong, and how could the system be changed to help protect other children? Those were the main questions behind the Turner Review and Investigation completed in September 2006 by Dr. Markesteyn, the Newfoundland and Labrador Child and Youth Advocate Delegate. The mandate of the review was to examine and investigate the circumstances surrounding Zachary's death.

Dr. Markesteyn noted that even with all the background on Shirley Turner, no one discussed the removal of Zachary at the time of his birth. He felt that, given the situation, a discussion should have been held regarding the custody of the child. Workers at Child, Youth and Family Services simply never raised the issue, yet should have. Dr. Markesteyn was shocked to learn during his investigation that while Turner was incarcerated awaiting extradition, she had left her 12-year-old daughter all alone in the St. John's apartment. Not only that, Child,

Youth and Family Services workers knew about the situation, and no one intervened to assist the child. He also noted that a man anonymously made complaints about harassing behaviour by Turner and no attempt was made to discuss the issue with Shirley. As well, Crown counsel was never notified of the complaints. Because there was already the possibility that a homicide had been committed as the result of a relationship ending, there were definitely grounds for a discussion with Turner.

In regards to Shirley being released on bail, Dr. Markesteyn offered serious questions about the validity of her release. Why was she let out on bail when part of the extradition case was that she was a danger to society? Turner's psychiatrist had already been massacred by the press and formally sanctioned for his surety for her bail. Dr. Markesteyn concluded his evaluation of the justice services by stating:

> "Had Turner not been released on 'bail' on 12 December 2001 or on 10 January 2003, my review would have been unnecessary. Zachary Turner would be alive today."

In his review of the Child, Youth and Family Services Act, Dr. Markesteyn found that definitions of "children in need" are not sufficient to enable workers to protect children properly. He recommended amending the act to be much more inclusive and specific in terms of the types of harm that can affect children, including the possibilty of harm by any adult, even one not directly responsible for the child. He also indicated that no case conference was ever held between the various community services. Had it been, Zachary's situation may have been more apparent.

Clearly, Turner's self-directed interventions with the social agencies dictated the agenda of the caseworkers. In this situation, the child's needs were overlooked in favour of trying to assist the mother. Constant attention was paid to the development of a plan for Zachary should Turner become incarcerated, but the procedure was completely driven by Turner, not by the CYFS worker. In highlighting this point, Dr. Markesteyn stated:

> "Nowhere did I find the question asked: What is in the best interest of an infant whose mother is facing a lengthy period of incarceration and court proceedings that are likely to be protracted?"

He went on to say:

> "My conclusion regarding my investigation of the delivery of Child, Youth and Family Services with respect to the death of Zachary Turner can best be articulated by addressing the central question: Should or could Zachary have been taken into protective custody?"

His answer to that was clear.

> "… Child, Youth and Family Services failed Zachary Turner by not knowing what could be learned,

and then not taking the necessary protective intervention steps."

Once it became clear that Turner was probably going to
be extradited, and once she had been incarcerated and put on
suicide watch, the CYFS workers should have become alert to
the change in Zachary's best interests. However, no investigation into Shilrey Turner was ever properly conducted, and
no assessment of the Bagbys was ever proposed. Therefore, no
proper evaluation of Zachary's best interests ever occurred. As a
result, a dangerous woman was allowed to maintain full custody
of an infant when she probably should not have been, and the
result was tragic.

~

Chapter Three

Ludmila Ilina

The two colleagues talked well into the evening of July 19, 1995. They talked about Ted Mieczkowski's recent trip, faculty gossip at the University of Manitoba and, most likely, their wives. After finishing a bottle of wine, Mieczkowski took his medication for jet lag and hopped on his bicycle to drive home. His colleague noticed that Ted was rather unstable as he rode away, but laughed it off as an effect of the wine. The following morning, Mieczkowski was found dead in his driveway, beaten to death. ∾

Zbiegneu "Ted" Mieczkowski was a geography professor at the University of Manitoba, and he was lucky enough to attend conferences all over the world. At one such conference, he met a Russian academic. Although she was 16 years younger than Mieczkowski, the two immediately hit it off. They wrote each other letters and postcards. She needed to use an English translator for her lectures and presentations at conferences, but would spend hours with a dictionary trying to send the perfect greetings to Mieczkowski. The pair fell in love and decided to get married. In 1989, Dr. Ludmila Ilina left Russia and immigrated to Winnipeg, Manitoba, to be with her love.

Ilina had a PhD in environmental and natural resources, and the University of Manitoba quickly offered her a position. Ted and Ilina worked closely together at the university. Although both travelled often for work, the pair seemed to have a close relationship. Working for the university forced Ilina to improve her English, though she still required a lot of time with her dictionary for formal writing. Incredibly intelligent, Ilina picked up the language quickly, even though she was in her 50s.

The couple lived in a modest bungalow in an excellent area of Winnipeg. Kings Drive, a short distance from the university, was just off the Red River and offered a family environment with good neighbours. The pair loved their home and neighbourhood. Neighbours reported the pair as being friendly and saw no signs of trouble between the couple. Although 71, Ted was often seen riding his bike and would even cycle to work when the weather was good. Neighbours were not aware that the couple did not share a bedroom or that Mieczkowski often slept on the couch.

In July 1995, Ted went on an extended trip to Poland and the Ukraine. He toured both cultural and academic sites. A few days after his return, Ilina was scheduled to leave for a conference in Vancouver, British Columbia. On the eve of her trip, Ted decided to visit a close colleague and friend. Ilina, needing to prepare for her trip, decided to stay home. Mieczkowski left on his bicycle.

Ilina packed her bags while Ted was gone. She put $300 Canadian and $1100 American in her wallet for her trip. She booked a cab for 5:30 AM the next morning to take her to the airport. Ilina took a sleeping pill and went to bed in her private bedroom with the understanding that Ted would wake her in time for her trip.

Mieczkowski had a great evening with his friend. Although he was still suffering from jet lag and insomnia as a result of his own trip, the medication seemed to be helping. As a frequent traveller, he had gotten used to the side effects. The two men shared a bottle of wine and ate cookies while they chatted. Ted's colleague recalls the professor leaving at about 9:00 PM and being a little unsteady on his bike. He never saw his friend alive again.

Police received a 911 call early on the morning of July 20. Dr. Ludmila Ilina called to report finding her husband in a pool of blood in their driveway. Police officers, firefighters and ambulance all answered her call. The first to arrive was a firefighter named Russell Bell. He and his crew arrived at 5:30 AM to find Ted Mieczkowski sprawled in the driveway with a bicycle on top of him. Ilina was sitting on the steps. Bell approached Ilina and asked her what happened. "I don't know," she replied.

She was understandably distraught and seemed to be in shock. He asked her if it was okay if they went inside. She agreed and led him into the house. She started showing them around the house but suddenly collapsed. She was unconscious for about 10 seconds, and then woke up and started crying. Someone called for the paramedics to come into the house to help Ilina. She told them that she was having chest pains, so they gave her some oxygen.

By 6:00 AM, paramedics had removed Ted's body from the driveway, and Ilina's health had stabilized. Police officers tried to talk with Ilina, but they had a hard time understanding her heavily accented English. She eventually had to show them her plane ticket and a prescription bottle of her husband's medication so the police could get the proper spelling of both their names. Police elicited the details of the couple's activities the previous night. Ilina told police that she woke up that morning without Ted's help. She went downstairs to look for him on the couch because he often slept there. Not finding him, she went outside, where she found him on the driveway under the bicycle. She got some water and poured it on his face but got no response, so she called 911.

Neighbours started arriving at the house to comfort Ilina and even brought her some tea. When Elaine Piamsalee arrived, Ilina fell into her arms crying. Everyone at the scene described Ilina as being in shock, distressed and frail-looking. Finally, the police put her in a car and drove her to the station.

They escorted her to a locked interview room and left her alone in the room for over an hour. At 9:45 AM, Ilina was told that her husband had died as a result of his injuries and that she was being charged with his murder. The police held her in the room for the whole day. Close to midnight, she was finally escorted to a cell.

Her time in interrogation was unpleasant. Ilina did not have anything to eat all day and says that she was never offered refreshments of any kind. She also says that she had a lot of trouble understanding the questions and her rights. She does not remember being offered a lawyer. When Ilina asked if she needed a lawyer, she was told that she didn't if she was innocent. She was put through three different interrogation sessions, each lasting between an hour and two hours. At 5:30 PM, after being held for almost eight hours, Ilina was strip-searched to check for any injuries that may have resulted from a fight. At about the same time, a friend of Ilina's had a lawyer call the precinct to talk to her. The lawyer, Radha Curpen, asked if Ilina was under arrest. Sergeant Robert Marshall, a homicide unit member, told Curpen that Ilina was not under arrest and that she would be able to leave once the questioning was finished. Of course, Marshall knew that Ilina had been placed under arrest at 9:45 that morning. When Curpen asked to speak to Ilina, Marshall told her that Ilina was too far away at that time. In fact, Marshall was speaking on a phone right outside the door of the interrogation room.

For four hours and 45 minutes after the strip search, officers sat with Ilina and prepared her statement and also recorded
a direct question-and-answer period. The entire time, the police
never recorded the interviews with Ilina, even though the interrogation room was equipped with both video and audio equip-
ment. Finally, close to midnight, Ilina was allowed to call a
friend. Thomas Henley says that the phone call from Ilina was
chilling. She sounded exhausted, tired and desperate. Although
she begged him to take her home, she was forced to stay the
night under arrest for her husband's murder.

The trial of the university professor garnered a great deal
of press. When Ilina went to trial, the courtroom was packed.
The case started off immediately with a voir dire into whether or
not statements given by Ilina, both oral and written, as well as
the pictures taken during the strip search would be admissible.
The judge viewed the circumstances of Ilina's interrogation and
decided that the statements were not admissible because of the
length of time Ilina was interrogated without food or drink, as
well as the blatant lies told to her lawyer. The judge did find the
results of the strip search admissible.

The case the Crown presented was entirely circumstantial. Police officers testified that they had arrived and found Ted
Mieczkowski lying in a pool of blood in his driveway. He was
dressed in a shirt and pants, which were not done up at the
waist. The pants also had bloodstains around the waistband. An
old bicycle lay on his body. Its tires were flat, and it was not the

same bike that he had ridden to his friend's home earlier. There was a pool of blood around his head as well as bloody footprints behind the car that was in the driveway and at the driver's side door. The prints were of shoes with a distinct waffle pattern. Although Ted had been wearing shoes with that style of sole, his shoes were clean and had not made the prints. As well, on the door of the car, the police found fibres that they were never able to identify. There was more blood on the front step of the house, including a print of a bare foot. The car in the driveway had a key in the door, as well as drops of blood around and under it. Police argued that the car had been moved to its location after the blood had fallen on the ground. Lying in a pool of blood was a man's wallet, empty. Mieczkowski's credit cards and driver's licence were found later in a cinderblock next to the house. Police found the bike that Mieczkowski had ridden earlier padlocked to a support of the carport. Beside the steps leading into the house, they found a piece of a green garbage bag with a staple attached.

The house did not show any signs of a break-in or forced entry and had not been ransacked. Inside the front door was a plastic floor runner that led to the living room. It had bloodstains, and there was a large pool of blood in front of the couch in the living room. There was a clear, wet stain along with the blood. Police officers stated in court that they thought it looked as if someone had tried to clean up the bloodstain using water. This issue became hotly contested during the trial and in the appeals that followed. The defence argued that the officers were not stain specialists and could not make statements as to whether or not the stain had been interfered with. The Crown argued that the officers were using their years of experience, not expertise, in forming their opinions. The judge agreed with the Crown and allowed the officers' testimony that they thought it looked as though someone had tried to clean up the blood. There was more blood on the walls and on the couch. It was obvious that the victim had been beaten in the living room and then moved to the driveway.

The police followed a blood trail to the basement and into the laundry room. There were more drops of blood in the laundry room, as well as a smear of blood on a detergent box on the dryer. When they opened the washing machine, they found some damp clothing that had already been washed, including the sweater that Mieczkowski had worn to visit his friend. As well, three large, green, plastic garbage bags and three other garbage bags all stapled together had been washed. Also in the load was a pair of black cloth gloves and a homemade balaclava. The Crown brought in an expert witness who examined the contents of the machine and found massive amounts of blood.

The Crown then brought in an expert on bloodstain analysis. Staff Sergeant Bruce Maclean felt that the stains in the living room were consistent with medium-velocity impacts. He also stated that the stains looked as if Mieczkowski had been left in the living room for a period of time and then moved out to the carport. Maclean did not agree with the officers' testimonies that the blood in the living room had been "cleaned up." Although he did not see the stain while it was wet, he saw no smearing around the edges, the sign of an attempt to clean the blood from the carpet. Another expert testified about the DNA of the blood. All the blood was a match to Mieczkowski, but one of the samples also included an unknown person's DNA.

The autopsy results for Mieczkowski showed that he had tried to defend himself, as he had some defensive injuries to his upper left arm. He had some blows to his face, which did not kill him, and more to his head, which would have rendered him unable to defend himself. In all, Mieczkowski had been hit with a "club-like weapon" as many as 19 times. The coroner stated that the force of the blows was not great and, if an appropriate weapon were used, it would not have taken a lot of strength to cause the professor's death. He also had marks on his skin from when he had been dragged out to the driveway. The coroner felt that the wine and medication in Mieczkowski's system were not enough to cause any kind of impairment, regardless of the testimony of his friend.

The Crown did not offer a motive for why Ilina would have wanted to kill her husband. They tried to introduce evidence of financial incentive, but the objections of the defence were upheld. The weight of their theory fell on the fact that no one else had opportunity to kill Mieczkowski, as there was no forced entry and no signs of ransacking, as would be present in the case of a burglary. The Crown proposed that Ilina and

Mieczkowski got into an argument, and she beat him with an unknown weapon. She left him in the living room while she created a "carrying sack" out of plastic garbage bags stapled together and moved him outside. Once on the driveway, she put the bicycle on top of him, took out his wallet and hid the cards to make it look as if a stranger had attacked him. At some point, Ilina got into her car and dropped the weapon, and possibly the clothes and shoes she had been wearing, into the Red River near their home. The prosecution argued that the bloodstains proved the car had been moved after the attack, and the garbage bags and clothes in the dryer were an obvious cover-up attempt. The stain on the carpet in the living room also pointed to Ilina attempting to clean up her crime.

The defence put forth a much different story. Ilina told police that on the evening of July 19 she packed for her trip and then went to bed. After booking a taxi for the next morning, she took a sleeping pill to help her sleep. She then went to bed and did not wake up until 5:00 AM the next morning. Surprised that her husband hadn't woken her, she went down to the living room to look for him. Apparently, as well as the couple having separate bedrooms, Ted often fell asleep on the couch. When she went downstairs, she saw the blood and followed the trail out onto the driveway. She ran inside to get some water, then tried to rouse him by pouring it on his face. When she did not get a response, she phoned 911. The fire crews and police arrived shortly afterwards. She informed them that she was missing all the money she had packed for her trip. Although at first she said that her wallet was in the bedroom, she later said it was in the bags she had packed and put in the living room.

The defence argued that the circumstantial evidence did not show that their client was guilty, but instead actually supported their theory. First, the unknown fibres from the door of the car indicated that an unknown person moved the car, not Ilina. The waffle shoe prints did not match any of Ilina's shoes. The police never found an object in the house that could have been used as the weapon. The empty wallet and Ilina's missing money indicated that Mieczkowski had been killed during a robbery. Also, there was unknown DNA in the blood sample taken from the driveway. Irrefutably, someone else had to have been there. Although Ted had defensive wounds, Ilina had no matching wounds that would show her as the aggressor.

The defence's theory was that Mieczkowski had difficulty riding his bicycle home as a result of mixing medication and wine. His friend even testified that Ted was somewhat unstable on his bike. At some point while driving home, Ted must have fallen and gotten a bloody nose. He got blood on his sweater, so he put the sweater into the washing machine. The defence did not attempt to explain the green garbage bags. After putting his sweater in the washing machine, Mieczkowski went upstairs and startled an intruder, who was stealing the money from his wife's wallet. A fight ensued during which Ted was beaten with an unknown object and killed. The defence noted that the Crown offered no motive for the crime, and Ilina actually had an absence of motive. She was deeply concerned for her financial security now that Mieczkowski was dead, and she had even mentioned it to police during her interrogation.

The jury did not agree with the defence's theory and found Ilina guilty of second-degree murder. Her lawyer immediately appealed on the grounds that the judge in Ilina's first trial did not instruct the jury properly as to the defence's theory or the importance of the missing weapon. Even though there was an intensive police search that included the area around the house and the Red River, the murder weapon was never found.

In March 2000, the Court of Appeal of Manitoba agreed with Ilina's defence team and ordered a new trial. After deliberating for three days, the jury returned their verdict—guilty of second-degree murder. Ilina was sentenced to life in prison with no chance of parole for 10 years. She was released pending appeals to both the Court of Appeal of Manitoba and the Supreme Court of Canada. Her team argued strongly that the DNA evidence along with the lack of motive, the wrongful admission of the "clean up" testimony by the officers and the missing money all supported the defence's theory of an intruder being involved.

However, in the Court of Appeal, the judge ruled that those pieces of evidence individually did not equal her guilty verdict, but when all aspects of the case were put forth, the jury reasonably found Ilina guilty. Both appeals were denied. Ludmila Ilina is currently serving her sentence at the Kingston Penitentiary in Ontario.

Chapter Four

Evelyn Dick

"You cut off his arms, you cut off his legs, you cut off his head. How could you, Mrs. Dick?"

By chance, some children out for a picnic found the torso on the side of a hill. At first they thought it was a pig. When they got close enough, the kids realized that pigs did not wear underwear. They did not know that their discovery would become one of the most sensational crime stories of their time. Then again, they had never heard of Evelyn Dick. ∾

THE FEMME FATALE

E velyn Dick was born Evelyn MacLean in Beamsville, Ontario, near Niagara Falls, in 1920 into a poor, far-from-perfect family. The family moved to Hamilton when Evelyn was a toddler. Her mother, Alexandra MacLean, was domineering and hated her low social status. Alexandra wanted more than the small, wrong-side-of-the-tracks house that her family of three lived in. She was sure that her beautiful daughter was the family's ticket to a more elevated position in society. She kept young Evelyn from playing with other children and attempted to control almost all of Evelyn's movements. Evelyn's father, Donald MacLean, earned a small salary working at the Hamilton Street Railway. Donald had a penchant for drinking and would swing from being benevolently generous to cruelly vicious in the blink of an eye. Alexandra and Donald often fought, violently on occasion, and they were constantly splitting up and getting back together. The unstable and controlling home environment resulted in Evelyn being socially awkward and emotionally needy.

Donald worked for the Hamilton Street Railway from 1924 to 1946. Working in the office, he learned the combination to the safe that housed the fare and ticket boxes. Unbeknownst to his employer, he regularly entered the safe and used duplicated keys to open the boxes and take whatever he wanted, though never enough to be noticed. His petty thefts were Evelyn's source of cash for new clothes and gifts. Classmates remember her always carrying around coins in her pockets. The MacLeans also bought a small home on Rosslyn Avenue, but Alexandra constantly complained that it was on the wrong side of the town's social scene.

Evelyn attended the Loretto Academy in the late 1930s. The private school educated the children of the town's elite. Tuition was expensive, and Donald MacLean earned only a paltry $1700 per year at the time. Luckily, he was making a fortune stealing from the company he worked for. Alexandra insisted on sending Evelyn to the school so that she would meet people who could help her advance socially. However, Evelyn had few friends. She tried to gain acceptance by throwing extravagant parties and buying expensive gifts for all the guests. She was so desperate in her attempts to buy friendships that she ended up being avoided. Classmates remember her wearing fur coats and, when she went out on dates, giving expensive presents as thank yous to her suitors.

As Evelyn progressed through high school, Alexandra encouraged her to keep company with wealthy men. Evelyn was often seen with some of Hamilton's most prominent citizens. In her late teens, she drove a fancy yellow sports car and had a variety of furs and expensive jewellery that had been given to her by her admirers. Classmates at Loretto eagerly discussed Evelyn and her many suitors, and she became the topic of constant gossip, a trend that would continue throughout her lifetime.

Evelyn's companionship with men resulted in a pregnancy, and at the age of 21, she gave birth to a daughter. To avoid the stigma of being an unwed mother, Evelyn invented a husband. She told people about Norman White, who was dutifully at sea with the Canadian navy. She began calling herself Evelyn White and gave her new last name to her baby girl, Heather. Of course, Evelyn's husband was wealthy, an elite member of high society and completely fictional.

Less than a year later, Evelyn was pregnant again. This pregnancy resulted in a stillbirth. When she became pregnant once more, again supposedly by Norman, who was still at sea, Evelyn's father put his foot down, refusing to have another baby in the house. As a result, Evelyn got an apartment of her own so she could continue to entertain male guests. Although she had never held a job, she somehow financed a very nice apartment in an upscale part of town. In fact, after the birth of Heather, Evelyn seemed to have a steady flow of money, which she often shared with her mother. When she met the landlord during the interview for the apartment, she referred to her pregnancy. She told him that the baby was already dead, and she would be going to the hospital to have it removed. She would, she mentioned, be bringing her three-year-old daughter with her to the apartment. The manager liked Evelyn and felt sorry for her, so he allowed her to rent the apartment. She furnished it and used it for social engagements, but did not move in until a year later.

Despite her statement to the landlord, Evelyn gave birth to a healthy baby boy in early September 1944. Peter White was a healthy and strong four kilograms. Evelyn had changed her story for the nursing staff. She claimed that she was a widow and that Norman was dead, lost at sea. The doctor thought that both Evelyn and the baby were healthy and scheduled routine follow-up appointments for Evelyn. Evelyn left the hospital a week after the birth with baby Peter. The nurses asked her to stay and see the doctor once more before she left, but she told them it was unnecessary. She departed with her baby and a small suitcase that her mother had packed for her. Three hours later, she arrived home—without the baby. Alexandra asked her where the child was, and Evelyn told her mother that she had given Peter to the Children's Aid Society for adoption. Relieved that she would not have to battle with her husband over the baby, Alexandra asked no more questions. Evelyn went to her checkups with the doctor and reported that baby Peter was doing very well.

In the summer of 1945, Alexandra MacLean decided to leave her husband once and for all. She knew that Evelyn had enough money to support them both, and the pair decided to move into the apartment that Evelyn had been renting for the past year. Later that summer, Evelyn met John Dick.

POOR JOHN

Mennonites fled Russia in the thousands during the 1920s, and John Dyck was one of them. He was 18 when he came to Canada with his family and set up a farming operation in southern Ontario. He lived with his mother and sisters, a grandmother and his brother-in-law, John Wahl. Dyck changed his surname to Dick, to be more westernized, and decided that farming wasn't for him. He moved to Hamilton and took a variety of jobs until he finally found work at the Hamilton Street Railway in 1943.

Co-workers remember John Dick as being pleasant and happy. He was a handsome, blond man, tall, with a strong

Eastern European face. He loved his friends and family and the occasional woman. He frequently went back to visit his family on their farm and to see his friend Anna Wolski, who had eyes for John herself. She was shocked when, out of the blue one day, he told her that he was married.

John was an unlikely match for Evelyn, far from her usual type. He had a low income, no assets to speak of and nothing financial to offer her. Many believe that he probably misled her when they met, inflating his wealth and status to equal hers. By this time, Evelyn had become a full-grown woman with deep, dark eyes and black hair. She was always perfectly turned out and often wore furs and expensive jewellery. She was petite but breathtaking. Hamiltonians remember her as looking like a movie star. She must have caught John Dick's eye while riding a streetcar he was driving. Evelyn undoubtedly led him astray with her story of widowhood. She told John that her husband had died in the war, but he was a stockbroker before he entered the navy, so she was left a fortune upon his death. She also very much needed a father for her daughter. Whatever the reasons, before a month had passed, the pair had decided to get married.

John did not meet Alexandra MacLean until days before the wedding. She was not impressed. Recently, Evelyn had been speaking to her of another man, Bill Bohozuk, as if there was an interest there. Suddenly, her daughter was marrying John Dick, a man Alexandra had never heard of. She was upset by the fact that he was a foreigner. She was also angry that all the work she had done to put Evelyn into an elite school and match her with Hamilton's wealthy ended with Evelyn marrying a streetcar driver. The day before the wedding, Alexandra tried to convince her daughter not to marry John. Evelyn stood her ground, and when her mother declared she would not attend the ceremony, Evelyn stormed out of the house.

The wedding on October 4, 1945, was small, with just the attendants and the bride and groom. John had called on a co-worker to stand with him at the wedding and asked the co-worker's girlfriend to stand with Evelyn. Since she was always busy courting men, Evelyn had never developed any female friendships. After the ceremony, the foursome had dinner at a Hamilton restaurant. The group broke up at about 11:00 PM and, much to John's surprise, Evelyn went home alone. The apartment, she explained, was too small considering that her mother and daughter were also living there. She wanted to get a house before they all moved in together.

I Do...or Do I?

A week after the wedding, Evelyn ran into Bill Bohozuk. The two had met a year earlier, when Bohozuk's girlfriend at the time introduced Evelyn to Bill. Evelyn encountered Bill again a few months before her wedding and gave him her phone number, but they never got together. When they met up again in

October, Bohozuk asked Evelyn out on a date. She eagerly accepted but did not mention that she was married.

Evelyn told Bill all about Norman, the naval husband who had left her widowed, and told him that she was using her maiden name now, MacLean. On their second date, she brought her daughter Heather along, and the threesome spent the day riding in Bill's car and playing at the park. After she told him a tale about her car being stolen, Bohozuk offered her his extra set of keys and told her she could use the car while he was at work.

Bohozuk worked a labour job at the Dominion Foundry. An avid rower, Bill was incredibly muscular and decidedly handsome. Everyone knew him to be affable, always up for a sporting event of any kind. He had a good job and a nice car—just the kind of man Evelyn liked to be associated with, even though she had just married John Dick.

Not long after receiving Bill's car keys, Evelyn showed up at the Dominion Foundry parking lot to borrow the car. The security guard was reluctant to let her take it, but when she produced the keys as proof of permission, he let her go. She brought the car back just before the end of Bohozuk's shift, and the two left together. That night, Bill and Evelyn went out with a group of friends and ended the evening sleeping together at Bohozuk's home.

John Dick, who had followed his wife that night, arrived at the Dominion Foundry parking lot the next day. He was crying and approached the same guard who had let Evelyn take the car the day before. John told the guard that he was Evelyn's husband and that he did not want her to be allowed to take the car again. When Bohozuk arrived for his eight o'clock shift that morning, John Dick approached him. John told Bill that Evelyn was his wife. Bohozuk, shocked, waved John off and started walking away. John followed him all the way to the entrance and finally left, crying. Bill left a message with Alexandra MacLean to tell her daughter to give him his keys back.

Later that day, Evelyn showed up again at the Dominion Foundry to borrow the car. The guard told her she wasn't allowed to take it. She left on a streetcar only to come back again later, this time followed by John Dick. The two fought, and then John took her by the arm and led her onto a streetcar. She returned the keys to Bill later that day. Bohozuk did not really see Evelyn again until late January 1946. During one of their dates in October, Evelyn had offered to loan him money if he ever needed it. In January, he damaged his car and borrowed $200 from her. He paid it back within two weeks.

John Dick did his best to keep his wife happy. Occasionally, Evelyn would sleep over at John's place, but most of the time, she shared a bed with her mother in her own apartment. John decided that the best thing for his marriage would be to buy a house. He tried to borrow money from both Evelyn and Alexandra, but both refused to lend him any. Evelyn found out that John was seeing other women, and three weeks into their marriage, Evelyn went to a lawyer and got a separation agreement drawn up. John refused to sign it.

At the end of October 1945, less than a month into the marriage, Evelyn bought a house on Carrick Avenue in Hamilton. John told people that he had given Evelyn part of the money needed for the down payment, but only Evelyn's name appeared on the title. The house was a beautiful three-storey brick home with a lot of room for the entire family. John could finally move in with his wife.

The arguments started immediately, both between John and his mother-in-law, Alexandra, and John and Evelyn. He was angry at not having his name on the title of the house and told everyone he could about the difficulties at home. John and Evelyn fought constantly about money, especially about John borrowing from Evelyn and Alexandra. Soon John started sleeping elsewhere again, sometimes for a few nights in a row.

Life at work began to be difficult for John as well. Donald MacLean complained to co-workers at the Hamilton Street Railway that John never had any money and was not taking proper care of his daughter. John and Donald fought frequently at work, the distraction causing John to have accidents with his streetcar. Both John and Donald received official warnings from the company via Raymond Castle, the superintendent of transportation, that if they did not keep their family business at home, they would be fired. They stayed off Castle's radar, but in one last fight, John told Donald that he knew about the money he was stealing from the Hamilton Street Railway. Donald threatened to kill John, who then contacted the Hamilton police. The police contacted Castle and informed him that Donald MacLean had threatened to kill John Dick and that MacLean was carrying a gun. Castle confronted MacLean but never saw a weapon.

In December 1945, John rented an apartment and began staying away from the Carrick Avenue house most nights. He moved out for good on February 3, 1946. The next day, a boarder moved in to help cover costs, and Alexandra and Evelyn began sharing a bed again. A month later, on March 6, 1946, John Dick did not come to work.

When John left Evelyn in February, he went to live with his cousin. Alex Kammerer and his wife, Ann, were not surprised when John asked if he could stay with them. They had known that trouble was brewing with the newlyweds for months. Ann dropped John off in downtown Hamilton on Ash Wednesday, March 6. He was in a sour mood, but Ann didn't push him for the reasons. Alex and Ann never saw John again. They thought he might have gotten back with Evelyn or found a hotel to stay in for a while and were not immediately concerned.

Also on March 6, Evelyn Dick showed up at the Grafton Garage to borrow a car from William Landeg. Landeg had bought the black Packard from Evelyn four years earlier but paid such a low price that he would let Evelyn borrow it whenever she needed to. She promised to bring the Packard back by 5:00 PM so that William could get home in time for dinner, but Evelyn did not return the car until 7:30 PM. In the meantime, she had tried to park the car in the garage at her home on Car-rick Avenue. Alexandra watched Evelyn attempt to park the car over and over in the garage, but the vehicle was too big. Alexandra told her that it would never fit into the garage, and Evelyn told her mother to mind her own business. In the end, Evelyn gave up and drove the car back to Landeg's garage.

William was gone by the time Evelyn brought the Pack-ard back, so she left a note with his mechanic. It read:

> I am sorry I was late Mr. Landeg, but my little girl
> cut her face, and I had to take her to the hospital
> for stitches. She got blood on your seat cover and
> our cushion. I will replace them later.

> Evelyn Dick

Landeg went to check on his car. It was covered in mud, even on the roof, and the right running board was damaged. When he opened the door, he discovered that the blanket from the front seat was missing, along with the seat cover. He put his hand down on the middle of the seat and noticed the seat was damp. He looked at his palm—it was marked with blood. Landeg was instantly worried about the little girl. The next day, he noticed something on the floor of the car. It was a sweater with some dark stains on it. Thinking the stains were oil, he threw the sweater into the corner of the garage.

On March 8, Alexandra and Evelyn's daughter Heather went for a walk. They went to the corner that John Dick would drive by on his streetcar, hoping he would blow the horn for Heather, as he usually did. That day, John was not driving. When Alexandra got home, she mentioned it to Evelyn.

"You'll never see him on a streetcar again, and it's not likely he'll bother me again," Evelyn told her mother. Alexandra was shocked by the coldness of her daughter's tone.

"What do you mean?" Alexandra asked.

Evelyn became upset. "Shut your damn mouth and keep your nose out of my business!"

Some Body's Found

The five kids were good friends. Faith and David Reed often hung out with Jimmie, Fred and Robert Weaver. They spent many days playing games on the street or having little adventures. At nine years old, Faith Reed was the youngest, and Jimmie Weaver, 12, was the oldest. On March 16, 1946, the group decided it was a good day for a picnic. They packed a lunch and, along with Teddy the dog, took a bus up to Mountain Drive Park. They were heading to Albion Falls, a roadside waterfall on Mountain Brow Boulevard. Along the way, Jimmie started fighting with Robert over a toy telescope and punched him in the nose. Robert turned and fled down the hill, followed closely by his younger brother, Fred. But they quickly turned and started running uphill again, screaming at the remaining three kids. Robert and Fred told the rest of the group that they had found a dead pig, or part of a dead man.

From where the group stood, they could all see what the boys were pointing at and decided to go and check it out. They carefully climbed down the steep incline, often having to hold onto the bushes and shrubbery that covered the hill. They got close enough to see clothing on the body, then turned and ran to the road to flag down a car. Having no luck, the kids formed a human chain across the road. Finally, a man and woman stopped. The children described what they had seen, and the driver went down to check it out. He came back immediately and told his passenger to get the police while he stayed with the kids.

The Ontario Provincial Police arrived at 11:00 AM. The torso was about a kilometre from Albion Falls. The arms and legs had been sawed off, as had the head. When the coroner turned over the torso, he noticed that someone had also tried unsuccessfully to cut it in half. The gruesome find was clothed in full-body underwear, missing the arms and legs. The body also had two bullet holes through the right breast. The area around the body showed signs that it had slid down the 45-degree embankment, but only for the closest few metres to the body. Someone had thrown the torso over the cliff rather than rolling it down.

Two days later, after the body had been hoisted off the hill using a special carrying basket and ropes, an autopsy was performed. Dr. Deadman, the aptly named provincial patholo-gist, performed the examination. He thought the body belonged to a man who had been killed about 10 days earlier. He noted that the arms, legs and head had been cut off with a saw rather than a knife, and there were several scratches on the torso. The amount of alcohol in the victim's blood indicated that he was most likely intoxicated at the time of his death. The two gun-shot wounds were caused by a single bullet—one wound was an entrance wound and the other was an exit wound. However, neither of the wounds would have been deadly.

The media swarmed the five kids. Newspapers from all over Canada took the children back up to the spot where they had found the body to take their picture. They were taken out for lunch and became celebrities, especially when rumours surfaced that the body belonged to mobster Rocco Perri. Perri had disappeared in April 1944. Three times before his disappearance, someone had tried to kill Perri, "King of the Bootleggers." But police knew the rumours were just gossip. This was a new body, not two years old, and it was hefty, not slight as Perri had been. The media didn't know at the time that John Dick would become much more famous than Rocco Perri.

GANG STORIES

Raymond Castle, the superintendent of transportation at the Hamilton Street Railway, became very suspicious when John Dick stopped coming to work. He approached Donald MacLean.

"Do you know where we can get hold of John Dick?" he asked MacLean.

MacLean replied testily, "I don't know a thing about him."

Castle decided to call the Hamilton police and report Dick missing. He gave them the address to John and Evelyn's home on Carrick Avenue. He also told Donald that the police were going over to Evelyn's home to look for John, and MacLean panicked. He called Castle a short while later and gave him the address of relatives, the Kammerers, that John had been staying with since leaving the Carrick Avenue house.

Castle sent a worker from the Hamilton Street Railway to the Kammerer's home, but when Alex and Ann reported that they had not seen John since March 6, Castle phoned the Ontario Provincial Police. It was the day before the children found the torso on the mountain.

When news of the body became public, Alex Kammerer contacted the police about his missing cousin. When the police came to visit him, he described John. OPP officers decided that Alex should go down to the station the next day to have a look at the body and see if it was John's. That evening, Alex got a call from John Wahl. John Wahl had married Dick's sister. Wahl was concerned about a phone call he had received from Evelyn Dick. She had telephoned him demanding to know where John Dick was because he owed her money. She even told Wahl that a judge had put out a search warrant on John, and that John had stolen money from the Hamilton Street Railway. Evelyn said that she had lent John $500, and he was going to pay her back using shares his mother owned in a canning business. Wahl was upset with Evelyn and immediately became worried about his cousin, so he called Alex Kammerer. Kammerer told Wahl about the body that had been found on the mountain and asked Wahl to come with him to the OPP station in the morning.

John Wahl, his brother Jake and Alex Kammerer all went to the station and then the morgue on Tuesday, March 19. Wahl had known Dick for years and immediately indentified the body lying on the morgue table as that of John Dick. John Wahl told the police everything he knew about Evelyn.

Charlie Wood, a long-time member of the Hamilton police, along with members of both the Hamilton police and the OPP, conducted a search of the house at 32 Carrick Avenue later that day. Wood asked Evelyn when she had last seen her husband, and she replied that it had been on March 4. He then told her that the body found on the mountain was John's. She stated, "Don't look at me, I don't know anything about it." Wood was surprised by her lack of emotion. He asked her to come to the police station for questioning.

Officers searching the house found a conductor's punch in the pocket of a fur coat hanging in the closet. Alexandra MacLean claimed the coat belonged to her. Upstairs, they found a conductor's moneychanger, a streetcar ticket box and $43.75 in unused tickets in a trunk. In Evelyn's purse, they found a picture of Bill Bohozuk and two bankbooks with accounts in Evelyn's name totalling $10,848. In the room at the Kammerer's home that John had been staying in, police found a scrap of paper with Bill Bohozuk's name.

Evelyn was taken to Hamilton Police headquarters to be interviewed. She sat in a small interview room in the detective's section, a room she would sit in again and again, telling version after version of her story. Her first interview was with Charlie Wood.

Wood asked Evelyn about the Packard. He had heard from Landeg about the blood on the seat and the note left by Evelyn. Evelyn told Wood the same thing she had told Landeg, that Heather had a cut and had bled on the seat cover, so she threw the cover away and brought a new one back for Landeg a few days later. He then asked her about John Dick. She replied, "Well, I know that he was running around with women, and in one instance, he had broken up a man's home in the city. I had seen him myself with other women."

She also said that she had gotten a call from a "member of a gang from Windsor." The gang member supposedly said, "We caught up with your husband. He was warned to lay off a friend of mine's wife, and he has left her in the family way. Now she is expecting a baby, so he paid us to put John out of business." She went on to say that the gang member had told her that she had to drive the Packard to the old James Street incline. Soon after she had arrived there, the gang member and another man arrived in a black Oldsmobile. A man got out of the car, dragging a heavy sack, and came over to her. He put the sack into the back of the Packard, against her objections.

When Wood asked her why they used her car, Evelyn said that the gangster had told her that everyone else in their gang was on a big job in Toronto. Wood then asked if Evelyn knew what was in the sack. She stated that the gangster told her it was part of John. She said the gangster made her drive to Concession Street and out towards Albion Falls. Just past Mountain Brow, she pulled the car over, and the gangster took the sack out of the car. He dragged the sack to the edge of the hill and rolled what was left of John down the incline. Then he got in the car, and Evelyn drove him back into town and dropped him off in front of the Connaught Hotel.

Wood, with years of interrogation experience behind him, found her story just a little too convenient. "So that was it. Just a matter of driving out there, meeting this man and letting him put the bag in the car with part of John in it, driving along to a bend in the road just before Albion Falls, and he throws it over the hill after he took the bag off it, and you drive back down the mountain, down Ottawa Street and leave him off at the Connaught Hotel?"

"He had to meet other people," Evelyn replied.

"Mrs. Dick, did you take any actual part in the murder of your husband?"

"No, no. I know nothing about where his legs, arms or hands are."

"But you know they are missing?"

"Yes."

Wood continued asking Evelyn questions about the gangster. She told him that he was probably carrying a gun, because they all do, and that he was Italian. When Wood asked her if there was anything else she could tell him about the death of her husband, she replied, "I am afraid to say too much. I will get a knife in my back or a bomb under my house." However, Evelyn agreed to take a drive to point out where she had stopped to let the gangster throw the sack and items of clothing from the car. Although they stopped at various locations, none of the items was found. Along the way, Evelyn began using the gangster's name—Romanelli—and when she got to the spot where the torso had been tossed, she told the officers that Romanelli had asked her to help him throw the body because it was heavy. When Romanelli pulled off the sack, Evelyn said she got sick and threw up. That night, police charged Evelyn with vagrancy, a charge that police often used to hold someone without much evidence, and she had to spend the night in a police cell.

Police impounded the Packard and picked up the dress that Evelyn said she had been wearing that night. They also visited Donald MacLean and took a .32-calibre Harrington & Richardson revolver registered to MacLean along with ammunition for the gun.

The next day, police picked up Bill Bohozuk. They had found a .32-calibre revolver at Bohozuk's home, which later testing showed had never been fired. When Evelyn found out that Bohozuk had been picked up, she decided to add something to her statement from the day before. She told Wood that Bohozuk hated John Dick, and that John had almost cost Bill his job by showing up at Dominion Foundries. She also said that Bohozuk had borrowed $200 from her to be used for "John to be fixed." When Wood asked her specifically what she meant, she replied, "Well, murdered, I guess. He was going to give the money to the gang that had come through Windsor."

She went on to say that Romanelli had told her more about Dick's death than she had said the day before. Romanelli apparently told Evelyn that Bohozuk had paid them to kill John. The gang had taken John drinking and then had gone driving afterwards, getting the car stuck. John got mad at the men, and they shot him through the head. After shooting John, they took him to a house and cut him up. When Wood asked if she knew where the limbs to the body were, she said that Romanelli had told her that they were burned in a furnace.

A BODY ABOVE

The police went back to Evelyn's home on Carrick Avenue. Detective Clarence Preston discovered a trunk in the attic. The lock was broken off. Preston asked Alexandra about it. She told him that Donald MacLean had come over the day before, drunk, and ordered her to give him something to break the lock open with. He went upstairs, and she could hear him pounding on the lock. After a while, the pounding stopped. She did not notice MacLean slip out the back of the house a while later. Preston examined the trunk but found only bath towels and books. He was much more interested in what Donald MacLean might have taken out. Preston then went to the basement and found a bushel basket for furnace ashes. The basket had a dark stain on it, and thinking the stain might be blood, Preston took it upstairs and out to the garage. After sifting through the ashes on the floor, he found bits of bone. Preston went and got Charlie Wood. Together they searched the ashes and the area in front of the garage. They found not only bits of bone, but also stumps of teeth and bloodstains on the garage wall. They decided to call in Dr. Deadman. He gathered up samples of the ashes and blood and determined later in his lab that they were pieces of human leg bones, upper arm bones and skull fragments. The blood from the bucket and wall was type O, the same blood type as John Dick's.

Police officers returned to Carrick Avenue on March 22 to search the attic. Detective John Freeborn found a locked suitcase. Alexandra said the key was lost, so they pried the case open with a screwdriver. A strange, strong smell came from inside the case, which contained a cement-filled box in a wicker basket, covered by a burlap sack. The cement had pieces of clothing sticking out of it. Freeborn immediately took the suitcase into evidence.

Back at the Central Police Station, Dr. Deadman supervised as the cement was chiselled away to reveal a brown skirt with Evelyn's name on it wrapped around the partially mummified body of an infant. The baby was clothed in a dress and sweater but had a piece of heavy string wrapped around its neck. The small body was badly decomposed and was missing its left foot and part of the ankle. It had been doubled up and forced into a zippered shopping bag.

Officers returned to the Carrick Avenue house yet again, where they met up with Donald MacLean and took him over to his house on Rosslyn Avenue to continue their search. Inside a gun locker in the attic, they found $4440 in cash. They also found stolen, unused streetcar tickets. They had discovered the proceeds of MacLean's career-long pilfering from the Hamilton Street Railway. Throughout the house, there were tickets stashed in pockets, coffee cups, paper bags and dresser drawers. As well, they found the stolen duplicate set of keys that MacLean was using to open all the streetcar and fare boxes. Then, in the cellar, they found John Dick's shoes, covered in mud, a butcher knife and a small carpenter's strip saw. Lastly, they found an August 5, 1944, edition of *Famous Detective Stories*. In it was a case that described how to dismember a body: "One by one, he cut away the arms, the legs, the head. He worked like a butcher— first the knife, then the saw. The floor was wet with blood when he finally finished." The victim in the story was then burned in a furnace to dispose of the evidence.

Officers arrested Donald MacLean, who was carrying $882.62 in cash at the time, and charged him with theft from the Hamilton Street Railway. Police later discovered bank accounts totalling over $60,000—a small fortune for the time. In all, it is believed that MacLean stole around $250,000 in the 22 years that he worked for the railway company.

When police approached Evelyn to ask about the bones in the ashes at her home, she changed her story yet again. She told of having sex with Bill Bohozuk in his home back in October of the previous year. She stated to the police that John had found out and approached Bill at work. Bill then told her "the gang is coming through Hamilton next week from Toronto," and they were going to "fix John." She changed her earlier story and said that John and Romanelli were downtown together walking towards Bohozuk's car. Bohozuk had told her that the gang intended to dope John's drink to get him to go along with them. Then, later that day, Bill called her to tell her they had "got" John. Bohozuk made Evelyn come to the Connaught Hotel to pick up a few of John's things in a paper bag. He then made her give him the Packard. He drove her home and left. Later, Romanelli came back. There was blood all over the car and part of a face and the limbs that they were not able to burn. Romanelli took them from the car and put them in the garage. Then Romanelli took her and the car to the Grafton Garage, and she was forced to take a taxi home. She told detectives that she thought Romanelli would come back to clean up the body parts, but he never did. Wood thought that

Evelyn was about to say she had burned the remaining parts, but was interrupted by a phone call informing him about the baby that had been found in the attic.

Wood told Evelyn that they had found a baby in a suitcase in her attic, wrapped in her skirt, and asked her if she could tell them about it. She replied, "I heard about it, but my lawyer told me not to talk." Wood left again and Evelyn was alone with Detective Preston. Evelyn, speaking to Preston, said, "I have something to say, but you must not tell my lawyer." She then proceeded to tell Preston that when she left the hospital with the baby, she met up with Bohozuk in his car. When Bill saw the child he said, "I will get rid of the little bastard," and strangled the baby with a blanket. She said that the next time she saw the baby was when Bohozuk brought it to her house encased in cement and told her to hold onto it until rowing season. Preston asked Evelyn why it was wrapped in her skirt, and she said that the cement had started to crumble, so she mixed more cement, wrapped the body in the skirt, and then poured the new cement over the package.

Wood and Preston both saw the pattern of Evelyn's confessions. Every time new evidence was found, she would change her story slightly to fit the new facts into the overall picture. "Every confession she gave was the true confession. And the point is, she did confess—she confessed half a dozen times and gave half a dozen different stories. She said she was going to keep telling and telling and telling until nobody really knew what happened," Clarence Preston's son told Brian Vallée for his book, *The Torso Murderer: The Untold Story of Evelyn Dick*. On Tuesday, March 26, 1946, Evelyn Dick was charged with the murder of her husband, John Dick.

THE CIRCUS TRIALS

A beautiful woman accused of killing her husband in a case that also involved a dead baby created a media storm unlike any before in Canadian history. Crowds gathered at the courthouse hours before Evelyn arrived for her first hearing. Police had to be posted at the doors to keep people out after courtroom capacity had been reached. The judge quickly remanded Evelyn into custody. Bill Bohozuk also was remanded that day, charged with vagrancy. His case was to be heard in a week. Two days later, both Evelyn and Bill were charged with murdering baby Peter.

Almost two weeks later, Evelyn asked to speak to Detective Preston. In a private room, she asked Preston when they would be bringing her father in. She told Preston that it was Donald MacLean who had loaned the gun to Bill Bohozuk to kill John Dick. She went on to say that MacLean had paid Bill to kill John after John had threatened to tell police about MacLean stealing from the Hamilton Street Railway. She claimed that Donald was getting drunk at the Balmoral Hotel while she and Bill drove up the mountain with John Dick. She stated that Bohozuk shot Dick on a side road. She told Preston that they had left behind some pop bottles that they had been drinking from on the side of the road. He asked her if she could accompany officers to pick up the bottles, and she agreed to go.

On the drive, Evelyn told Wood and Preston that John Dick's body had been in the Packard when she had tried to park it in the garage the night of the murder. "It [Dick's body] was left in the garage, and my father and Bohozuk looked after the disposition of it." She told them to stop where she thought they had thrown the bottles out of the car, but they found nothing. She then pointed out where the car had got stuck in the mud, then the place where John had been shot. "This is where Bohozuk shot John in the neck. The bullet came right out the right eye, and the blood splashed all over. He shot him again. The car was filled with gunpowder smoke. I was covered with blood, and I stopped the car. I got out the left front door, and Bohozuk got out the right rear door and pulled the blanket that was on the back of the front seat—pulled it over and wrapped it around John's head, and John groaned, and Bohozuk shot him again through the chest or stomach."

When the detectives questioned her story, knowing that John Dick had been shot from the driver's seat, she changed her story and said that Bohozuk was driving. Finally, she told the detectives that Bill had dropped John's body off at the Carrick Avenue house and came back later to carve up the body. The parts were burned at Bohozuk's home, Donald MacLean's home, and only pieces of flesh were burned at her home. When the detectives asked her if she wanted to put her new statement in writing, she told them that she couldn't because her lawyers told her not to say anything. Police decided to also charge both Donald and Alexandra MacLean with the murder of John Dick.

More than 100 spectators tried to get seats to Evelyn Dick's preliminary hearing, but few were allowed in. The judge decided that all the evidence would be heard "in camera," instead of open court and banned the public and the press. Evelyn at first refused to testify in court, but the judge, Magistrate Burbidge, ordered her to speak or be held in contempt. She then testified that Bohozuk was the father of her baby and that he had killed the infant. Bohozuk's lawyer, William Schreiber, immediately started attacking Evelyn.

"Haven't there been many men in your life?"

"A few."

"Quite a few. How many?" He pushed.

"I don't know."

The argument went back and forth that way until Schreiber said, "Give me the names of all the men you ever went out with." Magistrate Burbidge tried to interject, but Schreiber continued, "That you have had intercourse with and kept company with."

"The magistrate's son," replied Evelyn. And thus started the discussion of Evelyn's black book. Since Evelyn's teenage years, she had maintained a "black book" with the names of all the men she had dated and slept with. The book contained the names of the most prominent men, married and otherwise, in the city. She named stockbrokers, lawyers, military personnel, politicians and judges' sons. Because the hearing was in a closed court, the press and public did not hear the names of the men in the book. They were also never recorded in court documents by magistrate's orders. After two hours of closed-court testimony, the judge ordered Bill Bohozuk and Evelyn Dick to stand trial for the murder of their infant son.

Outside the courtroom, Bohozuk spoke to the press.

"I haven't one thing to do with this. Like my lawyer said, it's only the work of one person that keeps me here. I am innocent."

Next, Evelyn, Bill and Donald and Alexandra MacLean were brought before the court. After two days of testimony and evidence hearings, including the many statements made by Evelyn, Donald MacLean, Evelyn Dick and Bill Bohozuk were ordered to stand trial for the murder of John Dick. Alexandra was set free.

In the ensuing months, a media storm brewed, with Evelyn Dick at the centre. Kids began singing, "You cut off his arms, you cut off his legs, you cut off his head. How could you, Mrs. Dick?"

Evelyn Dick was a beautiful woman, and the idea of a female murderer, who had killed her baby no less, inflamed the public. People loved to hate her. Rumours of her sexual encounters abounded. Men in high positions were viewed with questioning looks. Just whose names were in her black book?

By October 7, the first day of the trial, the media had wound the public up into a frenzy, and thousands lined up outside the courthouse. The provincial Crown Attorney's Office had decided that Timothy Rigney would prosecute the case. He was the best prosecutor in Ontario at the time. Rigney chose to try Evelyn alone first, and then try Donald and Bill together afterwards. It was immediately apparent to everyone involved in the case that the judge, Justice Fred Barlow, favoured the prosecution. He often quickly dismissed defence arguments while giving the prosecution wide latitude.

There was a parade of witnesses: policemen from the scene where the body was found, detectives that had interviewed Evelyn and executed search warrants, Dr. Deadman, forensic experts and Ann Kammerer. The witness that caused the biggest stir was Alexandra MacLean, Evelyn's mother.

Alexandra admitted on the stand that she did not like John Dick and that she had arguments with Evelyn over her marriage to him. Rigney then asked about the day Heather and Alexandra went for a walk but didn't see John driving his usual route. Rigney asked her to recount the conversation she had with Evelyn when she returned home.

Alexandra stated, "I said to Evelyn, 'John was not on his car.' So she said, 'Well, it's not likely he will trouble me again, and you will never see him on a car.' I said, 'What do you mean? He is not finished?' and her face flushed. And the way she said it gave me the impression that something serious had happened. So she told me to shut my mouth and keep my nose out of her affairs."

When Rigney asked her to repeat what she asked Evelyn, MacLean stated, "I said, 'Why, there is nothing happened to him? He has not been killed?' And she said, 'Yes, John Dick is dead, and you keep your mouth shut.'"

Alexandra MacLean's testimony was like a nail in her daughter's coffin.

Throughout the trial, thousands of onlookers flooded the doors every time they heard that Evelyn was coming or going. The crowds only grew as the trial and the media storm continued. Crowds began forming at 6:30 AM, with onlookers hoping to catch a glimpse of Evelyn, now a celebrity. When Rigney closed the prosecution's case on October 15, Evelyn's lawyer, John Sullivan, did not offer any evidence for the defence. Evelyn would not testify. Closing arguments began the next day.

Sullivan pointed out the complex nature of the case to the jury. He stated, "It has many unusual angles and possibilities. It has attracted attention all over the country. The white light of publicity has beaten down on it. There have been a great many tales circulated of this event that have not come out in evidence. I wish you to wipe this gossip from your minds."

He also stressed that it was unusual for a mother to take the stand against her own daughter and suggested that perhaps Alexandra had her own motives for implicating Evelyn. He stated that it was suspicious that so much evidence that would point to Evelyn was just left lying around, and that Dr. Deadman had stated that the physical strength required to cut up a body was beyond Evelyn Dick's capabilities. "There is nothing presented here to show that this little woman could do it all by herself, although she may have known something about it afterwards. She could neither carry the body, nor cut it up… There is a great deal of evidence connecting her with the case, but not of the charge of murder."

Rigney confidently addressed the jury next. He said that Evelyn was responsible for the death of John Dick from the time she gave $200 for "a job that was expected to be done." He highlighted Evelyn's own statements to the police and Alexandra's testimony that Evelyn had told her John was dead before the torso was even found. He talked about Evelyn's history of lying—she had created a husband, constantly changed the story she told the police and had lied to John's family about the money he supposedly owed. He said that the only conclusion the jury could draw was that Evelyn was fundamentally involved in the death of her husband.

Next, Justice Barlow addressed the jury. He summarized the case and gave them instructions about convicting on circumstantial evidence. He told them that they must find

Evelyn guilty if they believed, beyond a reasonable doubt, that she had killed her husband or assisted in the murder.

Less than two hours after being dismissed to deliberate, the jury was back. They found Evelyn Dick guilty of murder. Evelyn quickly asked that her case be appealed. Justice Barlow noted her appeal and then sentenced her:

> "Evelyn Dick, the sentence of this court upon you is that you be taken from here to the place whence you came, and there be kept in close confinement until the seventh day of January in the year 1947, and upon that date that you be taken to the place of execution and that you be there hanged by the neck until you are dead. And may the Lord have mercy upon your soul."

The Court of Appeal granted Evelyn's appeal and gave her one major victory. It was decided that Evelyn's statements to the police were not made under proper instruction, since she was being held for vagrancy rather than murder. The appeal court granted her a new trial.

Evelyn's second trial was even more in the media spotlight than the first, now that she was slated to hang. Again people lined the streets hoping for the slightest glimpse of the murderess. Again Timothy Rigney was prosecuting, but this time Evelyn had J.J. Robinette to defend her.

In a surprise twist, the prosecution brought forth a witness, Frank Boehler, who said he had heard three shots fired, and when he investigated, he found a car stuck in the mud. In the car was Evelyn and the dead body of John Dick. Bill Bohozuk was standing beside the vehicle. Boehler stated that he helped pull the car out of the ditch and tow it to the top of a nearby hill. It was all too much for Robinette, who subjected Boehler to a fearful cross-examination. By the time Boehler stepped down from the witness box, he had virtually no credibility left.

Alexandra MacLean also took the stand in the trial against her daughter, and again told the story of Evelyn dismissing John Dick before the body had been found. This time she did not tell the jury that Evelyn had said that John was dead; she only stated that he would not bother her again. It did not have the same impact on the jury as before. In his cross-examination of Alexandra, Robinette hammered home points of Donald MacLean's access to the house and his hatred of Dick. As well, he brought up MacLean's pilfering at the Hamilton Street Railway and the fact that MacLean had hired someone to paint his furnace in the days after Dick's disappearance. Robinette clearly had his sights set on convincing the jury that Donald MacLean was the real killer. Again, Evelyn did not take the stand.

This time it took the jury five hours to reach a verdict. On March 6, 1947, Evelyn Dick was found not guilty of murdering her husband.

Evelyn was back in front of the court on March 24 on the charge of murdering her baby. Again, she would stand trial alone, separate from Bill Bohozuk. And again, Alexandra MacLean took the stand against her daughter. Alexandra told about visiting the baby once at the hospital, when the child was perfectly healthy, and then Evelyn coming home saying she had given the baby away. The most dramatic moment of the trial was when the suitcase was brought in as evidence, with the wicker basket and pieces of baby clothing. Alexandra admitted she had taken the same suitcase to the hospital full of baby clothes for Evelyn. The last time she had seen the suitcase, it had been full of books up in her attic. Again, Robinette tried to turn the jury's attention to Donald MacLean, highlighting his anger at Evelyn for bringing another baby into the house. In the end, though, the jury didn't buy it. After five hours and 20 minutes, the jury decided that Evelyn was responsible for her baby's death and found her guilty of manslaughter.

In a last-ditch attempt to save Evelyn from jail time, Robinette brought in a psychiatrist to testify that she was dimwitted and had a psychopathic personality. The judge did not crater. He sentenced Evelyn to the maximum allowable sentence—life in prison.

And Then There Were Two

Immediately following Evelyn's first trial, after almost a year of waiting in jail, Bill Bohozuk and Donald MacLean went to trial for the murder of John Dick. On Evelyn's day of testimony, she refused to be sworn in. Judge Urquhart asked Evelyn, "Do I understand that you refuse to give evidence and refuse to be sworn?"

"That's right," Evelyn replied.

The court tried again the next day, but Evelyn still would not be sworn in. After trying a third time, the judge ruled that a woman on death row could not be coerced into testifying and also felt that Evelyn did not want to ruin her chances of appeal. He ruled to hold over Bohozuk and MacLean's trial until after Evelyn's appeal was heard. However, after Evelyn was found not guilty, their trials were again put off until Evelyn was finished in the court system. Finally, after the manslaughter verdict came down, MacLean and Bohozuk got their day in court.

First, Bohozuk stood trial for the murder of Evelyn's infant. The prosecution's case was weak, and Bohozuk took the stand in his own defence. It only took the jury 23 minutes to find Bohozuk not guilty in the murder of baby Peter White. Two days later, he was back in court, this time with Donald MacLean, for the murder of John Dick.

A jury was chosen quickly, and the prosecution called Evelyn Dick to the stand. Again she refused to be sworn in. This time, Rigney submitted that without Evelyn's testimony, he had no case against Bill Bohozuk, so Bohozuk was free to go.

Donald MacLean was not so lucky. After the prosecution entered all the evidence found at the Rosslyn Avenue house, Donald decided to strike a deal with the Crown.

IN THE END

Evelyn was incarcerated for nearly 13 years. She spent 17 months in jail awaiting trial, and then 11 years and four months in Kingston Penitentiary. She was released on November 10, 1958, under the ticket-of-leave program, a precursor to the National Parole Board.

Evelyn Dick was given a new identity upon leaving prison. Although rumours and sightings have abounded in the 50 years since her release, her new identity has never been discovered. She was 38 when she left prison and, if she is still alive, she will be 88 on October 13, 2008.

~

Chapter Five

Rose Cece and Mary Taylor

The couple sat in the counsellor's office. Both women were homeless. Both were high on crack cocaine. And both were ready to end their lives with the small matching pocket knives they carried. One of them rubbed the other's back, trying to console her. The counsellor offered to "smudge" them, a traditional method of purification of the soul. One of the women did not feel she was worthy of the honour. The counsellor knew the women were serious about their suicide pact, so she sent them to the hospital. When the women arrived, they were told they would not both be admitted to the same hospital since they were lesbians. One of the women got angry. She told the staff that they would be sorry the next day. She was right. ❧

Mary Barbara Taylor and Elaine Rose Cece met in prison. Mary, 10 years younger than Rose, had always dated men. However, when she met Rose in prison, she suddenly found herself in love with a woman.

The two became inseparable at the Vanier Centre for Women in Milton, Ontario, which holds women in cottages rather than cells. Although the two women were not living in the same cottage, they had the same lunch hour. They began spending most of their time together, playing cards and watching TV. Soon, they were a couple.

Mary, a frequent offender, had over 70 convictions for everything from breaking and entering to assault. She had lived a hard 30 years. Even her conception had been brutal—she was the result of the violent rape of her mother, Gwen Herreman. Gwen tried to raise her child, but when drugs got in the way of parenting four years later, Mary went to live with her grandmother. The child suffered beatings and sexual assaults at the hands of her relatives and other men in her life and was left to fend for herself by age 11. By the time other girls her age were just starting to shyly smile at the boys in their grade eight classes, Mary was on the streets, prostituting herself to make enough money to buy whatever drugs she could get. By the age of 16, she was regularly shooting up cocaine and stealing or committing assault to get the money for her habit. Mary eventually married an abusive man. She gave birth to three children, apparently all from different fathers. Her husband, father to the oldest, died of AIDS, and she eventually lost custody of or gave away all her children. Her seemingly closest friend was her lawyer, David O'Connor, who defended her for over 20 years. She was in Vanier in 1997 because the convictions of the previous year were adding up. In June 1996, she had threatened an 85-year-old woman with a knife. Only five months later, she had beaten a 72-year-old man with his own cane to rob him of the $20 bill in his pocket. Taylor, it seemed, was a constant threat to public safety.

Rose, on the other hand, had led a relatively normal life. She had come close to graduating from high school, only four credits short, and had held a variety of jobs—school bus driver, nanny and trucker. Part Ojibwa, her culture was important to her. She grew up knowing that she was gay, though she had tried to date men for a short time. "It didn't do it for me," she told Christie Blatchford of the *National Post* in 1999. In fact, she slowly grew to hate men. She was serving 18 months at Vanier when she met Mary Taylor. Rose had succumbed to her inner ire when her long-time lover left her for another woman. She flew into a rage and kidnapped and assaulted the woman. As a result, she was charged and convicted of assault and forcible confinement.

While in Vanier, Rose and Mary made big plans, thinking about where they would live when they completed their sentences and what a happy life they could lead. When Rose was released, she moved out to British Columbia and rented a beautiful apartment in scenic Steveston, a small village on the edge of Richmond. Mary was supposed to meet up with her there when she got out. Instead, she chose to get high and was completely stoned when she called Rose. Mary begged her to come back to Ontario, so Rose packed up her few belongings, gave up her lovely new home, losing all the money she had paid in deposit, and drove back to Toronto. She met up with Mary at the Council Fire Toronto Native Friendship Centre, which offers counselling, treatment programs and cultural opportunities to the First Nations community. Because Rose arrived on Christmas Eve 1997, Mary thought of her as her Christmas present.

Soon Rose, who had never done drugs in the past, joined Mary on all-day, all-night drug binges. During the next eight months, the two lived on the street, Mary working as a prostitute to support the couple, and Rose becoming angrier and angrier at the men who were with her woman. The pair did drugs and drank incessantly. On August 4, 1998, they returned to Council Fire, declaring their intention to commit suicide. That same day, in another part of the city, Detective Constable Bill Hancox was at work.

Hancox had been with the Toronto Police Service for nine years. He had a wife, Kim, and a two-year-old daughter. Kim was eight months pregnant and, on the way to work, Bill had gone shopping for nursery furniture with his hockey teammate and co-worker, Detective Geoff Hesse. On August 4, 1998, Hancox was part of an undercover operation that was looking for a break-and-enter suspect so they could plant a GPS tracking device on the suspect's car. Usually, the team consisted of five officers, but this day, the team was inexplicably short two members. Regardless, Hancox was the lead, actively looking for the suspect, while the other two members circled the area.

Liz Jocko, a long-time counsellor at Council Fire, first saw Rose at the centre that morning as Cece was unloading food for the organization's food bank. Later that day, as Jocko was eating lunch, another worker in the centre, Mike Eshkibok, asked Jocko for some help. He had a suicidal client—Rose Cece.

Jocko took Rose to her office. There, Cece told Jocko the long story of her relationship with Mary Taylor and the addiction she now had to crack cocaine. She told Jocko she had been to other agencies looking for help to get off the drug that was taking over her life, but she "wasn't getting the help she was asking for." Rose started to cry when she told Jocko she had sold half of the "stuff" her grandmother had left to her. She felt she was letting her family down and was becoming completely consumed by shame.

Mary joined Rose in the room. She rubbed Rose's back and tried to comfort her lover. The couple had slept in a park the night before. They were hungry and desperate and had decided that night to kill themselves. They discussed jumping off a bridge or purposefully overdosing on heroin. Instead, they decided their small knives were the way to go. Rose showed Jocko a small pocket knife she was carrying. Mary brought out her matching knife. Jocko was deeply concerned. Although desperation and homelessness were hardly a new thing, this level of commitment to suicide was not the usual fare.

Jocko offered to smudge the women. Native peoples, along with many New Age followers, believe that a person cannot be healed until they are cleansed of any bad feelings, negative thoughts, bad spirits or negative energy. Using smouldering sage, smudging requires taking the smoke from the sage and rubbing or brushing it over and around the body—a sort of smoke bath. The smoke, as it rises to the Creator, soothes the aching soul. Rose at first refused the smudging. She felt that her body was not pure enough to receive the healing, because she had done cocaine that very morning. She felt she would be disrespecting the process. Jocko convinced her otherwise. Using an eagle feather, Liz Jocko wafted the sage smoke over Rose. She prayed to the Creator that Rose might find the "strength and encouragement to deal with her problems."

After the cleansing ritual, Jocko asked the women if they would be willing to seek professional psychiatric help to deal with their thoughts of suicide. The pair agreed they would. Jocko arranged for Rose and Mary to be driven to Scarborough Centenary Hospital and phoned the hospital to let them know that the patients were coming. While Mike Eshkibok went to get the van ready to transport the women, Rose and Mary left the room to get the two bags that held all their possessions. They were only gone for a few minutes, but when they returned, Rose was completely different. She was staggering and swaying. Her speech was slurred, and her eyes were glazed. Jocko, recognizing the obvious signs of intoxication, sniffed at Rose but couldn't smell any alcohol. She knew that the woman had taken

ROSE CECE AND MARY TAYLOR

something much stronger. Liz and Mary had to help Rose get in the van. Jocko did not hear from the women again until the next day.

Eshkibok dropped the women off at the hospital at 3:40 that afternoon, and they made their way to the emergency ward triage nurse.

Gloria MacDonald remembers Mary well because she did most of the talking for the pair. When Gloria mentioned that the girls must be good friends to know so much about each other, Mary told her that they had been lovers for the past year. The two were put in a quiet room to be assessed before going up to the psychiatric ward. Nurse Tamblyn remembers Rose lying on the couch, "gently rocking back and forth, crying to herself." She thought that the two women, listed as having no fixed address on their medical forms, were coming down off a drug high. They eventually went up to the 10th floor to the psychiatric crisis unit to see a psychiatrist, who agreed to admit the two women, but when he approached the staff to inform them, they reminded him of the hospital's unofficial policy of not admitting lovers together. When he returned and let the couple know that they couldn't both stay at the same hospital, that one could be admitted to Centenary and the other would be admitted at another hospital, Mary became enraged. She told him "that won't happen," then grabbed Rose by the hand and stormed off. She gave the nurses the finger as she walked by and yelled, "F*** you! You'll read about us in the paper tomorrow. You'll be sorry!"

The couple first left the hospital at 6:30 PM, but went in and out, to the bathroom and to the hospital's small drugstore, a few times. Finally, at 7:45 PM, they left the hospital for good, going past the parkade and heading north.

For the next two hours, the pair wandered the area aimlessly. They tried to beg for a ride out of the city, hoping to get to the country and away from the drugs. They called their relatives to say they had reached the end and were going to commit suicide. Their relatives didn't believe them.

June Martin was sitting in her car in the hospital car park at about 9:30 PM when there was a sudden rap at the window. She jumped in her seat and saw the big woman's face. June rolled down her window and snapped at Rose, "You scared me!"

Rose leaned in and said, "We're stuck. We're stranded." She begged June for a ride, but Martin turned her down flat. The pair decided that they needed a plan, so they decided to get a knife to help them steal a car so they could get out of the city. Mary went into a local grocery store and stole a 12-inch butcher knife. Then the pair walked to a strip mall that was kitty-corner from the hospital they had left two hours earlier and went into a phone booth to stake out a car. They agreed that if they found a car with a woman in it, they would hold her up, drive away with her in the car, and then leave her safely on the side of the road. If it was a man's car, he might not be so lucky.

Meanwhile, across the street from the strip mall, Detective Constable Bill Hancox was just being relieved from his post as the "eyes"—the lead officer most closely watching the suspect. He had been outside the suspected break-and-enter ringleader's apartment for hours, waiting for him to return. The operation was part of a long-term sting on the group, and the team had just gotten a warrant allowing them to put a GPS tracker on the man's car to try to track his movements.

Being on a stakeout is stressful, often boring, and Hancox was likely weary. He stopped at the strip mall and went into Becker's, a small convenience store. Mary and Rose apparently saw him enter the store. One commented to the other that he was a handsome man. They didn't realize he was an undercover police officer, since he was not in uniform. Hancox bought a pop and a Snickers chocolate bar before going back out to his unmarked van. Rose and Mary approached him. Hancox had a reputation for being genial, even friendly, to people on the street. As usual, he chatted with the couple for a minute and then sent them on their way. Mary offered her services to him, but he told her he was a married man. He got in the van and pulled over to another spot in the parking lot to eat his snack.

Rose and Mary walked around to the back of the van. This would be their target. Mary began to lose it. She started urging Rose to get the man out of the vehicle, but Rose wanted to steal an unoccupied car instead. Mary started calling Rose a "pussy." Mary told her to get the van. "Prove you love me," she told Rose. "F*** it! Use the knife."

Rose approached the window of the van. She put her left hand on the half-open window and reached in with her right, stabbing the knife 12 centimetres deep into the police officer's chest. The knife went into Hancox's left lung, ripped his pulmonary artery and vein, and came to rest on top of his heart. He grabbed the knife, and Rose and Mary fled. When Hancox pulled the knife from his chest, a splash of blood flew across the van's visor. He stepped out onto the pavement, reached for his radio and, barely audible through the gurgling of blood, stated, "I'm stabbed." He held on to the radio for 15 seconds.

Most of the transmission was unrecognizable to Detective Steve Pattison, who was watching the apartment across the street. Hancox leaned back into the van and turned the engine off. He reached up and tried to turn on the dome light, but he didn't make it.

Detective Pattison was at the van within 60 seconds of Hancox being stabbed, yelling "Officer down! Officer down!" into his radio. Bill Hancox was lying on his back beside the van when Pattison arrived. "Hang on Billy! I'll get help," he told his friend and partner. Hancox's eyelids were heavy, and moments later his eyes closed. Pattison looked for a pulse. It was barely there. He tried to give Hancox CPR by breathing into his partner's mouth, but the air came right out in a spray of blood from the hole in the man's chest. He tried compressions, and again was spattered with blood. Sergeant Geoff Howell, a uniformed member of the force, arrived on scene and pushed Pattison out of the way.

Howell knelt on the pavement beside Hancox's head. He saw blood clots forming in the detective's nostrils, and Hancox's mouth was full of blood. Howell rolled the man's head into his own lap and attempted to clear his airways, but there was too much blood. There was only the faintest trace of a heartbeat.

The fire department, ambulance attendants and other officers all poured into the small parking lot. Everyone tried to help "Billy from hockey," but it was no use. There was so much blood that the paramedics couldn't even find the chest wound at first. They finally found the hole in Hancox's shirt and tried to put plastic bandages on the sucking wound, but there was too much blood, and the bandages couldn't stick. They got Hancox into the ambulance and headed off to Sunnybrook trauma centre in the city. The medics tried hooking up three suctioning machines, but they all filled with blood within a minute. At 11:02 PM, less than an hour after being stabbed, 32-year-old Detective Constable Bill Hancox was pronounced dead.

Around 10:00 PM, Isabelle Noulet was coming home from bingo when she saw Rose and Mary. She lived in the same building that the police had under surveillance that night. "I didn't like the looks of them," she said. Rose was leaning against the wall of the apartment building, just outside the ramp to the parking garage, and Mary was waving her arms up and down in the air. Noulet thought that Taylor was "giving her shit." She parked her car, went upstairs to her apartment and almost immediately heard the sirens. She ran back down to see if the women were still there, but they were already gone.

During the next few hours, the women made their way over to Mary's brother's home. He was living in a bedroom in the basement of a rooming house in the east end of Toronto and at the time was also housing his mother and her boyfriend. The girls came in and woke up Mary's brother, Danny Herreman. Mary immediately said, "I've got something to tell you guys. Rosie just stabbed someone." Danny didn't believe his sister, so they turned on the television. Sure enough, at the bottom of the screen, on the tickertape announcing the news, it stated that a police officer had been rushed to the hospital with "vital signs absent."

Rose and Mary started to panic, screaming, "We didn't know he was a cop!" Mary's mother, Gwen Herreman, told the women to turn themselves in. Instead, they wanted to run up North, or anywhere else out of the city. There was a lot of crying and wailing, but eventually the group fell asleep in the early hours of the morning. When they woke up again, they quickly turned on the TV. Hancox was dead, and the police were looking for a male suspect. It calmed the women down a bit.

The girls stayed at the house until early afternoon, when Danny asked his sister to leave. He did not want their trouble in his house. Mary started crying and screaming at him, "I'm your sister!" But it was no use. The pair left and spent the night on the streets once again. After they had gone, Danny called his brother and his father and got their advice as to what he should do about the women. They felt he should turn them in. Mary and Rose returned to Danny's the next day. They hadn't been able to sleep on the street and wanted to get some rest before they headed on their way. He told them that they couldn't stay but gave them his last six dollars. After much arguing and yelling, the pair left for the last time.

Danny called his brother again. This time, his brother set up a three-way call with 911. Danny told the operator that his sister and her girlfriend were the ones responsible for the death of the officer and that they could be found near his house. He collected $1000 as a reward for his information. Rose and Mary were soon taken into custody.

On October 4, two months after Bill Hancox's death, Rose Cece and Mary Taylor stood in a courtroom in Toronto and pleaded guilty to manslaughter. However, John McMahon, the Crown prosecutor, rejected their pleas. He stated in court that the couple "intended to cause the death of Detective Constable Hancox" or, at the very least, "intended to cause him bodily harm that they knew would, or was likely, to cause death." It was the difference between second-degree murder and manslaughter. The women would go to trial for the more serious charge of second-degree murder.

The highly publicized trial took the jury through 11 days of testimony. Officers that were on scene the night Hancox died gave testimony about their partner's last moments. Constable Craig Stewart, the blood spatter expert, testified to the bloodbath of a scene that he had encountered. A fine pink mist of blood that Hancox had breathed out while sitting in his van was evident on the roof and on the steering wheel. Blood was all over the seat, the door, on the keys, the armrests, the police radio, around the dome light and in a strip across the visor. There were pools of blood outside the van where Hancox had stood next to the vehicle, and then near the back tire, where he finally fell to the ground. The forensic pathologist, Dr. Martin Bullock, described the injuries to Hancox's lung and his heart, how the blade had slipped between the second and third ribs, ripping the upper lobe of his left lung and cutting the airway and arteries. By moving and possibly by pulling the knife out, the detective had exacerbated the wound and made it wider. Dr. Bullock told the court that there were no defensive wounds, indicating the victim's unawareness of the attack.

Detective Pattison described hearing the garbled message on the radio and rushing across the street to find his partner near death. He told the court that the team was missing two members, but did not explain why. Other officers at the scene described their roles in the attempts to save Hancox's life. The officers were stoic and unemotional while testifying. Only when McMahon asked them did they reveal that they loved their co-worker, played hockey with him, spent time with him and his family. They stated that their training kicked in for them when they tried to help Bill Hancox, but it couldn't prepare them for the pain afterwards.

Mary Taylor's brother took the stand. He told the court about the two women arriving at his house, begging for his help, and how he turned them in. The women's lawyers tried to show him as cold and calculating, but the damage had been done.

Then Mary's mother took the stand. She told the court that Mary confessed that Rose had killed Hancox, but that they didn't know he was a police officer. Mary's lawyer, David O'Connor, pressed Gwen Herreman. Didn't they have a fight that night? Didn't her daughter call her a "pill-popping drug addict"? Wasn't she a horrible mother, passing her daughter off to any family member that would take her? "You hate your daughter, and you want to get her, don't you?" O'Connor asked her. "I do not hate my daughter," she replied. Both family members' testimony showed the hard life that Mary Barbara Taylor had lived.

Witnesses presented testimony as to the pair's actions that day—that they had been using drugs, their suicidal thoughts, the row at the hospital. The defence wanted to show that Rose and Mary were at the end of their mental ropes and were slowly breaking down. They hadn't meant to harm anyone else—they were up against a wall. They certainly hadn't planned to kill a police officer, one of the main reasons for the second-degree murder charge. When the prosecution rested, both defence teams chose not to call any witnesses or present any evidence.

During his closing remarks, Crown Prosecutor McMahon held up a replica of the knife that Rose had used that night. "They weren't using this to give the man a shave," he stated. He talked of a cold-blooded attack. "The man was executed in a planned ambush," he told the jury. He finished his three-hour speech by stating, "Bill Hancox paid the ultimate price for doing his duty," and challenged the jurors to do theirs.

Marshall Sack, Rose's lead lawyer, was up next. He told the court, "Ms. Cece doesn't seek an excuse or ask you to condone what she did… No socio-economic deprivation, no movement of the stars, no disenfranchised aboriginal background, no amount of intoxication—nothing—justifies what Rose Cece did." However, he argued, the jury had to decide her criminal responsibility. He argued that she was not in a mental state to form the intention to kill. Her main goal was not murder. She was pushed by her lover to try to steal a van using the knife as a weapon. Not knowing that Bill Hancox was a police officer, her actions resulted in his death, but she did not intend to kill anyone. She was high on drugs and had an "ultimate disintegration of the thought processes of a human being." She should be found not guilty of second-degree murder. Sack spoke for less than an hour.

It took the jury less than two days to find both women guilty of second-degree murder. At the sentencing hearing, Bill Hancox's wife, Kim, read her victim-impact statement. "All my dreams and hopes died with Bill in that parking lot," she stated. "Rose Cece and Mary Taylor may as well have plunged the same knife into my chest. In a way, I guess they did—they hacked my heart to pieces." She wrote about the new baby that had been born a month after his father's death and how difficult it was to raise the children without their dad. "My daughter will never have that golf lesson with her dad. My son will never play that hockey game with his father. I will never be able to fill his shoes."

When the judge asked the two women for a statement. "I'd just like to apologize to the Hancox family," Taylor stated. "I can only imagine the pain they're going through," Cece practically whispered to the court.

Judge Watt then sentenced both women to life in prison. However, Cece, who actually killed the officer, could apply for parole in 16 years. Taylor had to wait 18. David O'Connor was furious. "It's just not right that the person who was the aider and abettor gets more than the person who did the actual killing," he told the press after the sentencing. However, what upset the lawyers even more was that they had been rejected when they asked for a stay of proceedings as a result of finding out that Detective Pattison had deceived the court. His testimony had not been entirely truthful.

Where had the two other members of the undercover team been when they were supposed to be supporting Hancox, Pattison and Hesse? Kim Hancox had been asking that question since the night of her husband's death. It came to light that the officers were in a bar—drinking.

The news broke in the time between the jury verdict and the sentencing hearing. Constable Larry Smith, a regular member of the undercover team, and Detective Elmer Manuel, the technical support officer, did not meet the rest of their team on August 4, 1998, at the strip mall for the surveillance operation. Instead, they spent some time at Manuel's house and then watched Manuel's son's hockey practice before going to a bar.

At one bar, they had four rum and Cokes and a beer, according to the bar receipt, and more at the next. They were sitting with drinks in front of them at a country and western bar when their pagers went off telling them that their teammate had been stabbed. Constable Smith then had the audacity to claim 12 hours of overtime for his "work" that night. His supervisor even approved the hours.

David O'Connor petitioned the court, stating that Pattison had not told the truth on the stand. He had known the officers were not where they were supposed to be, and that the Toronto police force had withheld evidence, therefore denying his client a fair trial. The judge denied the stay of proceedings and sentenced the women. Rose and Mary appealed, but the decision stood.

As for the officers, Constable Smith, an 18-year veteran, lost only 12 days' pay—six for drinking on the job and six for neglect of duty. The Toronto Police Association, calling the decision politically motivated and nothing but a minor labour dispute, appealed Smith's sentence. Manuel, taking the easy way, retired before he could be sentenced. The supervisor for the unit, Superintendent Paul Gottschalk, also received a reprimand for not passing the information up the chain of command when he found out where his officers really were that night. There was talk of laying criminal charges against Pattison and Hesse, the two officers who did their jobs, and tried to save their partner's life, for not telling the whole truth on the stand. Those charges were never laid.

Rose and Mary did not stay out of the media spotlight for long after their sentencing. In January 2000, two months after they were sentenced for killing Bill Hancox, they were found guilty of assault. While in prison, they beat up another inmate, Marcia Dooley, who was in protective custody awaiting trial for allegedly killing her seven-year-old son. Cece and Taylor started asking her questions about the killing, and when she wouldn't answer, they grabbed her hair, pulled her off her chair and threw her to the ground. Other inmates surrounded the woman so she couldn't get away. Mary and Rose received 30 days for the assault, to run concurrently with their other sentences.

Later that year, after they gave an interview from prison, public ire was raised when it was revealed that the two spent their days together playing cards, smoking and watching TV. They told journalist Christie Blatchford that they kissed each other goodnight before going to sleep in separate cells. The idea that a pair of murderers got to spend their sentences together outraged many and, in the end, the women were separated and sent to prisons in different parts of the country. Rose Cece will be eligible for parole in 2015, Mary Taylor in 2017.

Chapter Six

Diana Yano and Danielle Blais

The woman moved quietly through the holiday condominium located three hours from Calgary. Her husband was out enjoying an afternoon round of golf while she stayed with her two preschool children. She filled the bathtub, then she brought her two children into the bathroom and drowned them. Her husband discovered the bodies when he returned from his afternoon of leisure and called 911.

Across the country in Montréal, another woman also held her son's head underneath water to end his life. Her son was autistic. The president of the Montréal Autism Society came to the defence of the woman and later offered her a job. ∾

DIANA YANO

Hiroshi and Chiyeko Tomimoto were two of the 23,000 Japanese Canadians who were rounded up during the early 1940s and forced to live in an internment camp. Ian MacKenzie, the federal cabinet minister from British Columbia, stated at the time, "It is the government's plan to get these people out of BC as fast as possible. It is my personal intention, as long as I remain in public life, to see they never come back here. Let our slogan be for British Columbia, 'No Japs from the Rockies to the seas.'"

Japanese Canadians were taken from their homes and businesses, allowed to pack only one suitcase of belongings, and transported to meagre and often dangerous camps. Chiyeko and Hiroshi, both in their early 20s, were moved from their British Columbia homes to a camp near Calgary. After World War II ended, the family chose to stay in that area because their house had been seized and not returned, and they moved into the city of Calgary. But the pain of the camp and the humiliation and degradation caused by the Canadian government put down deep roots in the couple's psyche.

The couple had four daughters. Diana, the youngest, was born on May 24, 1962. Diana and her sisters, not having been victims of the internment camp, had no problem making friends with other children. When Chiyeko and Hiroshi found out their daughters were befriending non-Japanese Canadians, they were irate. They felt that the girls had disrespected the family by turning a blind eye to the treatment "Canadians" had inflicted on their parents. The Tomimotos, feeling shamed, threatened to commit *seppuku*, a type of ceremonial Japanese suicide. The shame that her parents felt severely affected then seven-year-old Diana. For the rest of her life, she strived for perfection in an attempt to regain their respect.

Diana became a high achiever. Constantly receiving top grades, she graduated near the top of her class. She went on to university, where she took two degrees simultaneously, nursing and music. The stress of the heavy course load sent her into a deep depression. When she was 19 years old, she attempted suicide for the first time. She slashed her wrists but was discovered before she bled to death. Not long after, suffering in shame for the failed attempt, she again tried to commit suicide by driving her car off an overpass in Calgary.

Although she failed in both attempts, the accident left lasting damage to her spine. She had to undergo serious back surgery that required a long period of healing. As she became more and more depressed, she started to show signs of psychosis. The psychosis led to delusions that lasted for over six months. Her family, trying to use cultural-based healing, refused medication for their daughter. They took care of Diana, and she seemed to recover. However, because of her history of mental problems, she could never go back to nursing. She decided to go into engineering instead.

Diana graduated as a chemical engineer from the University of Calgary with top grades and exemplary evaluations. She landed a job with the prestigious TransCanada Pipelines. As well, she continued her music training and earned certification from the Royal Conservatory of Music as an ARCT level piano teacher.

Diana loved being outdoors, playing golf and tennis, and going skiing and hiking. She also volunteered a great deal of time with her church and the Pet Access League Society, a group that organized animals to come into hospitals to help cheer up patients. She met and married Craig Yano, and the couple continued to live in Calgary. They were well off, both having high-paying jobs in the booming Calgary economy, and they decided to buy a timeshare at the Mountainside Vacation Villa in Fairmont, British Columbia. The couple had two children, and Diana was a devoted mother. She appeared to have overcome her depression and delusions.

In 1989, when Diana was 27, her mother died of breast cancer. Diana was devastated by the loss. Eight years later, while nursing her second child, a boy, she discovered a lump in her own breast. With a three-year-old daughter and an infant son, Diana's first thought was that she had to survive.

She appealed to her doctors to give her an experimental, extremely harsh form of chemotherapy to treat her cancer. She did not want to die and abandon her children. The chemotherapy was toxic. It killed her bone marrow, almost killing Diana at the same time. She underwent a bone marrow transplant to bring her back from the brink of death.

The strong chemotherapy also affected her mind. Possibly because of her history of depression, the drugs brought on another bout of the illness. This time, she was prescribed antidepressants. However, in January 1998, Diana was feeling better and chose to stop taking her medication. She said that she wanted to be self-reliant, so stopped her depression treatment abruptly.

Three months later, she was again deeply depressed. As well, the psychosis was back. Her sisters took her on a holiday to British Columbia to try to cheer her up, but things only got worse. Again, Diana attempted suicide and ended up in the Foothills Hospital in Calgary. Psychiatrist Dr. Elisabeth Zoffman said, "Unfortunately, Mrs. Yano continued to want to stop the medication, displaying an intense belief she could correct the problems herself."

Diana refused to take her antidepressants and antipsychotic drugs. Again she plummeted into a deep mental illness, becoming hypermanic and going on wild spending frenzies. At times Diana became extremely agitated or overtalkative. She would spin around a room, completely overactive, unable to sit down, yet she still refused to take the medicines she was prescribed.

By early summer of 1999, Diana was again delusional. She heard voices, sometimes believing the devil was speaking to her. She suffered from wild hallucinations and began to believe she was damaging her children. Diana started to think that the only way her children would be safe was if she killed herself.

The family went on vacation to their timeshare in Fairmont, BC, in June 1999. Planning to spend a week, as usual, they were looking forward to time outdoors. On June 29, Craig left his wife and two children, Brittany, five, and Joshua, three, to go golfing for the afternoon. When Craig returned at 4:00 PM, he was unprepared for the scene that awaited him. He walked in to find both his children dead in the condo's bathtub. He immediately called 911, but it was too late. Emergency medical personnel attended the scene, but it was obvious that the children were long gone. The police were called. They arrived at the condo quickly, and by 5:30 PM, Diana Yano had been arrested for killing her two children.

She was brought before a court in nearby Cranbrook. The presiding judge ordered Diana to undergo a 30-day psychiatric assessment in a Vancouver mental hospital. She was also placed under suicide watch because of both her history and her crimes.

Friends rallied around both Diana and Craig, some driving from Calgary to help Craig pack up the children's belongings from the condo and transport them back to Calgary. Laurie Neske, Diana's close friend, said that the case was "so tragic. Diana's world was her children. This is something you can't ever fathom. I don't know how [Craig] can cope."

Craig Yano gave a statement to the media a few days after the killings. In it he states:

> "A terrible tragedy has occurred in my family. My two most wonderful, most beautiful, most precious children, Brittany and Joshua, are gone. The grief and suffering felt by myself and my family are beyond words and is something that I would hope no parent should ever have to feel.... Two years ago, Diana suffered a serious battle with cancer that left her susceptible to extreme depressions.

No one can fully understand what has happened in these past few days. However, what is known for sure is that Diana was a very loving mother to our two kids and always wanted the best for them."

In court, the Crown chose to call only one witness—Diana's psychiatrist, Dr. Zoffman. Dr. Zoffman testified to his patient's long history of mental instability and told the court that at the time of the murders, Diana was suffering from a bipolar disorder that caused her moods to fluctuate between euphoria and extreme depression. She told the court that Diana had progressed to the point where "at the time of her children's deaths, the only way she saw to save them was that she had to drown them to send them to heaven." Dr. Zoffman portrayed Diana as a loving mother who was now in deep grief. The judge found Diana Yano not criminally responsible for the deaths of her children, and she was remanded to a psychiatric ward in a hospital in Port Coquitlam, near Vancouver. In March 2000, Diana was released, and she moved back to Calgary with her husband. Craig Yano was always steadfast in his support for his wife.

Diana threw herself back into volunteer work, both at church and with the Pet Access League Society. A memorial was erected for the children on Shawinigan Drive in southwest Calgary—two hawthorn trees planted side by side with a commemorative plaque dedicating the trees to the memory of the children.

On August 18, 2006, at the age of 44, Diana Yano jumped to her death from the third floor of a parking garage at a Calgary-area hospital.

~

DANIELLE BLIAS

Three years before Diana Yano killed her children during a psychotic episode, another woman drowned her child in the bathtub. Mental illness was also an issue, but this time, the mother was sane.

Danielle Blais was a single mother when her five-year-old son, Charles, was diagnosed with autism. Autistics often have impaired social interaction, problems with verbal and non-verbal communication, and unusual, repetitive or severely limited activities and interests. Charles was attending a specialized school in Montréal, and though his autism was fairly severe, he was able to perform basic activities with other children. He tended to go from extreme hyperactivity to extreme withdrawal. When Charles' father left the family, Danielle went into a deep depression. She started having trouble with childcare, as all the babysitters that she hired quit after a short time. She finally lost her job at a radio station because of all the time she had to take off work to resolve childcare issues.

On November 6, 1996, Danielle Blais found dealing with Charles and his condition more than she could take. She filled her bathtub and held six-year-old Charles underwater until he drowned. She wrote a note stating how much she loved Charles and describing her depression. "Misery, isolation, poverty, sadness. I feel all alone, and I can't do it anymore." She then tried unsuccessfully to kill herself by slashing her wrists.

Police charged her with first-degree murder, though the charges were later reduced to manslaughter. She pleaded guilty. However, her biggest supporters came from the most unlikely place.

Peter Zwack, president of the Québec Autism Society, publicly stated that Danielle should not have faced first-degree murder charges and that she definitely should not have to go to jail. "Her life was a nightmare. She was all alone, and that would have made things more impossible," he told the *Montréal Gazette*.

Carmen Lahaie, president of Montréal's Autism Society, also rallied to Blais' defence. She called out to the media to encourage support from other parents of autistic children. She raised money for Danielle and held demonstrations to support her. Lahaie, in a statement to the media, said that Charles was "happy now." Lahaie even went to court to testify for Blais. She told the court that it was a huge burden to take care of an autistic child; others could not understand unless they lived through it. She failed to mention that, with treatment, many children with autism can improve and even lead relatively normal lives as adults. But even more shocking to many was the offer Lahaie extended to Blais to hire her to work at the Montréal Autism Society part time to assist other parents dealing with autistic children.

The crown asked for Danielle to serve three years in prison to dissuade other parents from taking such matters into their own hands. In the end, Justice Jean B. Falerdeau accepted Lahaie's testimony and stated in his summary that Blais "did not want to leave her son alone or impose on others the burden of taking care of an autistic child." He also wrote, "I have much difficulty believing prison will dissuade someone who is sick." He added, "Clearly, the defendant doesn't represent a danger to society. She could even work to help other parents of autistic children."

Falerdeau sentenced Blais to a 23-month conditional sentence. She was required to spend 12 months at the Thérèse Casgrain residence, a sort of halfway house, and she served the rest of her sentence in the community. Carmen Lahaie stayed true to her word and hired Danielle as a representative of the Montréal Autism Society. When asked by Michelle Dawson, a Montréal autism rights activist, why she would hire a woman who couldn't cope with the pressure of having an autistic child to help other parents learn to cope, Lahaie told her, "You can't understand. Our children have ruined our lives."

In 2003, as part of the opening address to the conference Autisme 2003, Lahaie stated, "It is time to…cure and prevent this plague once and for all. People with [autism] will never be able to speak up for themselves, so they wait and suffer. We, parents and professionals, have to do it for them." (translated)

Individuals, autistic and not, called for the resignation of Carmen Lahaie in response to her calling autism a plague, but

Lahaie remains as president of the Montréal Autism Society. In a letter to the Collège des Médecins formally laying a complaint against Dr. Victor Goldbloom, who repeated Lahaie's comments, Michelle Dawson, a diagnosed autistic, stated, "Being described as a plague by an eminent doctor can only harm autistic people, who are citizens, who are taxpayers, who contribute greatly to society in spite of facing intolerance and ostracism. We are not a plague.... The real mystery is why we are not seen as human beings with rights." The College chose not to investigate her complaint.

Danielle Blais only worked with the Montréal Autism Society for a short time. Her whereabouts today are not known.

~

Chapter Seven

Jane Stafford

"Every emotion possible was felt in that courtroom at that moment, yet I couldn't move. I was in shock. I said to myself, 'Thank you, Lord, for the miracle you just performed.' I just couldn't believe the verdict. Alan had prepared me for the worst. I didn't know how to accept the best. I'd never once allowed myself to believe the verdict might be not guilty. I killed someone, and they were telling me I was free to go. I didn't know how to react."

–Jane Stafford, as told to Brian Vallée in *Life With Billy*

BECOMING BILLY

Billy Stafford was born on February 13, 1941. He claimed he was sent by the Devil, or even was the Devil, and told people he was born on a Friday. He wasn't. He came from a family with lots of children and a good income. His father ran a successful junkyard business in

Liverpool, Nova Scotia. Although his parents were strict with Billy, as he grew into a teenager, he could not be controlled and became abusive towards his parents, especially his father. Billy's temper and quick use of his fists became famous in the area as he grew into an adult.

When he was 21, Billy married his pregnant girlfriend, Pauline Oickle. Shortly after the wedding, he started abusing her, hitting her with beer bottles, broom handles and anything else that was convenient. He would punch her in her face and body until she was bleeding. Even tiptoeing around Billy did not help. "He could be nice one minute, and the next minute, he'd turn right on you and just start beating you for no reason at all. He would really get wild-looking. His eyes would be just glaring, and the spit would fly and froth from his mouth." Pauline reported to Brian Vallée in the book *Life With Billy*.

When Billy was drunk, he was even worse. One night, after drinking with Pauline's mother, Billy cornered Pauline and started kicking and punching her. Left, right, left, right, left, right, over and over until Pauline's face was unrecognizable. Pauline escaped from Billy when he started to tire and went to her uncle's house, running through the snow in only a night-gown and slippers. As soon as she got to her uncle's, he took her to the hospital. The doctors thought she had been injured so badly that she would lose the baby she was carrying. Somehow the baby survived. Photographs of her face and body were taken at the hospital, and Pauline pressed charges against Billy. Billy's father came to his son's rescue and convinced Pauline that

Billy would never hit her again if she would agree to drop the charges. Pauline agreed to do so as long as Billy signed a peace bond stating he would stop being abusive to her. Within two weeks, the beatings started again.

Once children were added to the relationship, five altogether, he started beating them as well. "He never treated the children with love at all. I'd say from the time they were six months old, he started beating them. When you put them to bed at night, they didn't dare cry, or he'd go up and beat them, right in the crib." Billy would sit all the kids on the stairs and put lighted cigarettes into their mouths. After the cigarette burned down, he would make the kids eat the butts. He would even put his children up against the side of the house and throw knives at them to see how close he could get without hitting them.

Pauline finally decided she had to leave when Billy beat her youngest daughter particularly badly one morning before leaving for work. He took the girl, a toddler at the time, into the backyard, held her facedown by placing his foot on her back and beat her with a rocker from a wooden rocking chair. He didn't stop until the girl messed herself. Then Billy walked over to his wife and kissed her goodbye. Pauline knew she had to leave, so she packed her things and fled with the children to Ontario to her cousin's home. When Billy returned from his work on a fishing boat two weeks later and found Pauline and the children gone, he was furious. He went straight to Pauline's mother and tried to beat information out of her. She wouldn't tell him anything. Pauline was granted a divorce on the grounds of cruelty after six years of hell with Billy.

At work, Billy was not a nice person, either. He worked as a merchant seaman. He had tattoos on his arms and was nearly two metres tall. He weighed 115 kilograms, sometimes more, and wasn't afraid to use his size to intimidate and bully others, both on and off the boats. During his career, he was blacklisted from various boats, usually for mutiny, and mysterious events would happen while he was on board. On one occasion in 1974, when Billy was 33, a young man named Jimmy LeBlanc went overboard while working on the same boat as Billy, the *Mersey Enterprise*. The rumour, as Billy later admitted to his wife, was that Billy threw Jimmy overboard after a heated argument. Police believe that Billy scared his fellow crewmen into silence, so charges were never laid against him for Jimmy's death. The company never gave Jimmy's family an explanation of the tragedy, and they were not able to get a death certificate. Jimmy LeBlanc is listed as missing at sea.

By the time Billy met Jane Hurshman in 1975, he was 34 years old. He had a failed marriage and a failed common-law relationship that ended after his girlfriend fled for her life to Calgary with Billy's baby. He had six children that he was not supporting and a string of exes hiding for their own safety. But Jane Hurshman, unaware of Billy's past, saw him as her ticket out.

A DIFFICULT START IN LIFE

Jane Hurshman was born on January 25, 1949, in the small town of Brooklyn, near Liverpool, Nova Scotia. The town was situated right on the coast and relied heavily on the ocean for its survival. The Hurshmans were poor, like many in the small town, and lived in a large home, but without heat, running water or a bathroom. Jane's father, Maurice, worked at a sawmill nearby, and he would carry scraps of wood home from work to help heat the house in the winter. But the cold always came in. Maurice left for Korea as part of the Armed Forces when Jane was one year old and fought there for 19 months. He came home in 1952 but stayed with the army as a chef. As was typical of family life in the army, the Hurshmans moved around a lot.

In Truro, Nova Scotia, Jane's older brother got a room of his own, and Jane shared a room with two younger sisters. It was in Truro that Jane first saw her father beat her mother. He started drinking a lot and became more and more unpredictable and irritable. Jane remembers sitting unnoticed at the top of the stairs and watching her father and mother fight.

In 1957, when Jane was six, the family moved to Gagetown, New Brunswick. Jane became close friends with a neighbour girl, Valerie, and often escaped to Valerie's peaceful home to avoid the violence in her own. When Jane was at home and the violence would start, she would lead her siblings down to the basement and sing to them to cover the sounds. Spousal violence was not uncommon on the base, and neither were loud parties and heavy drinking. It was a scary but normal life for Jane.

The family was transferred to Germany when Jane was in grade seven, one month after Valerie's family moved there, and her father's heavy drinking continued on the other side of the ocean. There was even a truck that delivered beer right to the front door of the family home. With his ration cards, beer was cheaper than pop. Valerie's family did not drink and gave Maurice their ration cards so he could buy even more alcohol. Loud music and drinking sessions with friends were an everyday occurrence at Jane's house in Germany. One day, Jane came home to find her father screaming at her mother to clean up the vomit that he had drunkenly spewed all over the living room. Jane waited outside for the commotion to end, when suddenly the front door flew open. Maurice looked right at his daughter and said, "I hate you." He stormed off, and for a long time afterwards, Jane thought, "If my own father hates me, then who will ever love me."

Things changed one day when Jane was 14. She came home to find her mother in bed, too sick to get up. When Maurice came home and found his wife in such a state, he took her to the hospital. Gladys Hurshman was bleeding extensively from a tubal pregnancy. The doctors were not sure she was going to survive. Jane stayed home with her siblings and lay with them when her father came home that night. She heard him whispering in the living room and realized he was praying. She overheard him begging God to let Gladys live and made a deal with God that if his wife survived, he would never hurt her again. Suddenly there was a knock at the door. Someone was urging her father to return to the hospital—they did not expect Gladys to make it through the night. Maurice rushed out. Jane never forgot her father's prayer. Gladys Hurshman did survive, and Maurice, though he often drank heavily and swore at his wife, never hit her again.

Jane was 15 when the family moved from Germany to Winnipeg, Manitoba. It was cold and snowing, and the family had to live in a small motel for months before they found a home. Jane's mother started working, so Jane looked after the children. She wasn't able to go to school on the base because the family lived so far away, and her grades started falling. She had always been an "A" student, so she got the shock of her life when she received a failing grade on her report card. She learned that all the kids who returned from Germany failed because the school considered them to be a year behind. It was too much for Jane, so when some friends of her parents moved back to Nova Scotia, Jane asked to go with them. Little did she know that she would be again living in a drunken, abusive home. The first chance Jane had, she moved to her grandmother's home in Liverpool. She thought she was safe there.

Jane and her grandmother lived downstairs in a house that they shared with Jane's uncle James. James lived in the upstairs part of the house with his new wife and child. The home was another "party central." James worked on the scallop draggers, and often his fishing and drinking pals would drop in. One of these friends became Jane's lover.

Jane's grandmother took exception to the relationship because the man was nine years Jane's senior, and told Jane to stop seeing him or she would send Jane back to live with her parents. So Jane started to see her boyfriend on the sly. One day, after returning from school, she found her diary open on her bed and realized that her grandmother knew everything. Feeling violated, Jane packed all her belongings and left.

She moved into the tiny, crowded home of her maternal grandparents. There, her boyfriend was allowed to come over anytime and often drank with Jane's grandfather. Two months after Jane turned 16, she became pregnant. The couple got married in April 1965. Jane's parents did not attend the wedding.

Jane's new husband quickly lost interest in her for everything except sex. When the baby was born in October, he did not even come to the hospital. Jane's new baby, Allen, became her life. The couple stayed married but lived separate lives for years. Loveless, mechanical sex produced a second child, Jamie, in 1972. In the meantime, Jane's husband had been keeping himself busy with a mistress on the side. He had taken pictures of her naked, legs splayed, with objects in her, and he hung the photos up at his job. Jane's husband was even arrested once for drinking and driving while out on a date with his mistress.

Although she was disgusted by the pictures and crushed by her husband's infidelity, there was a new baby on the way, so Jane decided to try to make her marriage work. Her husband had other plans. He came home drunk one night, carrying a bottle of alcohol. Jane told him it was either her or the bottle. He kissed the bottle and told her she was out of luck. Jane packed up her belongings and her children and left. She moved in with her parents, who had returned to Nova Scotia.

A few days after leaving her husband, Jane went to see him to discuss a divorce. Allen, then 10 years old, did not want to leave his school in the middle of the year, so Jane agreed to let him stay with his father. She tried to get welfare but couldn't until she was legally divorced. During a meeting with a legal aid lawyer, Jane's husband secretly came and took Jamie, the youngest child, who was being looked after by the welfare director's secretary. When Jane returned, the welfare director shrugged and told her, "Well, since you don't have any dependants, we can't help you." Jane knew she had been set up. She ran to her sister-in-law's home and banged on the door. Although she could hear Jamie crying for her, no one would open the door. She finally had to leave with her child still crying inside the house. She returned to the lawyer and was told that since her husband did not accept the divorce, and since he had as much right to the kids as she did at that point, there was nothing she could do. She either had to have grounds for divorce or get her husband to agree to the divorce. She knew a way to get both. She thought of an acquaintance of her husband, Billy Stafford.

Jane approached Billy, only wanting to have sex with him to force her husband to give her a divorce. But she soon became enamoured with him, and Billy and Jane started living together in January 1976. He was romantic, always telling Jane that he loved her, and he treated her like a queen. She thought of him as her knight in shining armour. He promised her that she would never be hurt again. Little did she know that the worst was yet to come.

Jane's Safe Haven?

While Jane's ex-husband was busy poisoning her sons against her, Jane was creating a new life with Billy. She felt safe and loved. Although there was drinking, it was all very social, and Billy always took Jane with him wherever he went. The couple eventually moved into a small and very dirty old house that they rented for $25 a month. Jane worked hard to make it beautiful, all with Billy's loving support. However, she missed her children tremendously. She would even drive to their school at lunchtime and secretly watch them on the playground. Billy told her that eventually her ex-husband would find them to be too much work and give them back. She prayed for it everyday.

Billy wanted to have a baby of his own and told Jane to stop taking the pill. Although she didn't want another child, she wanted to make Billy happy. She got pregnant in August 1976. Suddenly, Billy's whole attitude towards her changed. He made her change her name, unofficially, to Jane Stafford, though the two did not get married. He seemed to feel that with her now pregnant with his child, he owned her, and the true Billy emerged. As her belly swelled, he refused to take her out. He stopped making love to her and became verbally abusive.

Billy was out on the boats when Jane went into labour. Baby Darren was born, and two days later she had a tubal ligation. A day after Billy returned from the boats, he came to visit. He was cold and uncaring. He told her that the baby was her responsibility and acted as if it had been her idea to get pregnant. When he found out about the ligation, he was enraged and told her that she was "no f***ing good" to him anymore.

Later, when he came to pick Jane up to take her home, he was no better. Even though the doctors had told her to rest as soon as she got home, Billy forced her to clean up the terrible mess he had made while she was in hospital. She couldn't believe that the lovely home she had worked so hard to create was in such bad shape. Billy had vomited on the bed and not cleaned it up. There were bottles and cigarettes everywhere. No dishes had been done, and Billy had left a bucket full of human waste in the bedroom because he couldn't be bothered to go outside to use the outhouse. She looked around at the mess, and Billy said to her, "Well, what the hell are you waiting for? Can't you see all the work that needs doing around here? Put that little bastard in the crib and get busy." She worked all day, drawing water from a well and bringing the heavy buckets up to the house, which had no running water. She was exhausted and in pain when she finally crawled into bed that night. Billy left for the boats a few days later.

Things did not get better when Billy came home. He immediately demanded sex from his wife. Jane had just had her stitches removed, but Billy did not see that as an excuse to avoid sex. "I haven't touched you since you started getting big, and now I want it." He forced her to go to the bedroom and strip for him. When he came in, he started criticizing every aspect of her body. He took her roughly, then rolled over and went to sleep.

After a couple of months, Jane and Billy had to move from their house when the landlady decided to move her mother into it. They lived with Billy's parents for a short time, and then moved into a home in Bangs Falls, Nova Scotia. Jane got a job in a nursing home to make some extra money for herself and Darren. As soon as she got paid, she would buy groceries and pay the bills. Billy would steal whatever was left over and go drinking.

In November 1977, things got worse. Jane came home after a day of shopping with some chicken to give to Billy and a friend, both of whom had been repairing the kitchen sink's plumbing all day. Billy demanded to know where Jane had been and ordered her to feed him. She gave the men the chicken and put Darren to bed. She was sitting out on the veranda after Billy's friend left when Billy came out. He grabbed her hair and pulled her into the house. "You f***ing whore! You slut! You tramp! I saw you giving Richard the eyes. You just bought that chicken to impress him didn't you?" he shouted at her. Despite her pleas, Billy slapped and punched her. It was the first time he had ever beat her. The next day, he was apologetic and promised it would never happen again.

Jane began to doubt herself. She didn't know if she had done something to deserve the beating and decided to be more vigilant about monitoring herself. However, every time Billy had a friend over, the situation repeated itself. Jane began staying in the bedroom if there were guests in the house, but the beatings continued.

Billy caused trouble on the fishing boats as well and ended up getting blacklisted after being charged with mutiny for holding a knife to a shipmate's throat. The RCMP served Billy with papers charging him for the incident. He slammed the door in their faces and then pointed a rifle at the officers as they went back to their squad car. When Billy went to court, the charges were dropped. Everyone was too afraid of Billy Stafford to testify against him, just like the time that Jimmie LeBlanc went missing.

With no job, Billy relied on Jane's paycheque. He said to her, "Well, old woman," the term he used to refer to her, "you're working now, so I don't need to work. You can look after me." Although he spent his days at home, Billy would not take care of his son, luckily for the child. Darren spent his days at the home of the neighbours, Marie and Morton Joudrey. The couple were open and loving and easily accepted Darren into their home. They had a son about the same age, and the two played together while Jane was at work. Darren loved staying there and was terrified when it came time to go home.

In the book, *Life With Billy*, Jane recounts Billy's horrible treatment of Darren. "Darren was just something to be abused and used and taught to make it through life as a man." Darren, from the age of six months, was not allowed to cry. "Through the middle of the night, as any baby does, he would cry... Bill used to go to the crib, and I'd never hear another word. But I wasn't allowed to get up and go to him. I used to wonder all night long, is he dead?" Billy also beat Darren from a very young age. One day, when Darren was three, Jane was working in her garden. Billy shouted at her to summon her into the house. He told her there was a mess to clean up. The "mess" was Darren, lying beaten and bleeding on his bed, covered in excrement. He had raised welts on his body, head to toe, from the broken mop handle that Billy had used. "His tiny body was quivering like a wounded animal. He had defecated during the beating, and there was blood and feces all over the bed and floor." Jane began to cry. Billy punched her in the face.

"Get this f***ing mess cleaned up, old woman. We're going out. And get the kid dressed. He's going, too." Jane did as she was told, and the little family drove down to visit the next-door neighbour and Jane's friend, Margaret Joudrey (no relation to Marie and Morton Joudrey). They all went for a drive as if nothing had happened.

Another time, Darren fell off his chair and banged his mouth so hard on the table leg that his teeth cut through his lip. When Billy came home, he asked Darren if he had cried. Darren admitted that he had. Billy punched Darren three times in the face, full force, sending blood flying. He warned him never to cry again. Darren was three years old. Billy would often pick his son up by the hair and hold him up in the air, sometimes putting a knife to his throat. He would force-feed the child, making Darren eat as fast and as much as he did. Darren occasionally threw up from the feedings and was forced to eat the vomit. Billy often reached out at the table and punched Darren or hit him on the head with a cup or a plate. It was impossible to predict when Billy would strike. He would hold Darren upside down by the feet and point a rifle at the child's head, threatening him to be a good boy or he would blow Darren's brains out. If Jane ever complained about Billy's treatment of their son, Billy would beat her, sometimes to unconsciousness. Darren was not allowed to play with his toys, and Billy often broke them or ran over them with the truck while Darren watched. Darren was so frightened of Billy that he would shake the whole time Billy was around.

In January 1982, sixteen-year-old Allen, Jane's son from her marriage, decided to live with Jane and Billy. Jane did not want Allen to come; she worried about how Billy would treat him, but Billy insisted. Predictably, Billy started hitting Allen, too, so the boy tried to avoid Billy as much as possible. Billy began treating Allen and Ronny Wamboldt, a boarder living in a shack on the property, like his personal slaves, forcing them to work for him, carrying wood and fixing things. He often beat them. Ronny was frequently intoxicated and couldn't remember many of the beatings Billy administered to him. But he never retaliated.

After being unemployed for a few years, Billy started to work off and on with various work programs and on the boats. He frequently got into trouble or would quit or lose his job. He eventually got involved with drugs and started bringing them into Canada on the gypsum boats he worked on. The family had periods of peace while he was gone, but things always turned hellish when he came home.

On day, Billy shot at Jane as she bent over to put wood in the stove. The bullet hit the wall, centimetres from her head. "Don't worry, old woman. If I had wanted to hit you, I wouldn't have missed," Billy said to Jane with a laugh. When the shock subsided, she told Billy she was going to leave him. He told her that he wasn't worried. He would shoot her family one by one until she came back. She believed him and had never felt more stuck.

Billy also frequently attacked or threatened the lives of many people in the small community. He shot at day labourers who were working in the area, threatened to kill a man who confronted him about shooting his dog and sped up to hit pedestrians crossing the street. He was feared by almost every-one in town. He would occasionally be charged with something and have to go to court, but was always let off with a fine. Even the police were afraid of Billy. Eventually, no officer wanted to step foot on his property because Billy had sworn he would shoot at any that tried. They knew he was telling the truth.

The police had their suspicions about Billy's drug business. As Billy travelled to Europe and South America, drugs started becoming more prevalent in the small town. Jane says that Billy first brought in just marijuana, but then graduated to hashish and acid. He not only sold the drugs, but used them as well. Things got even worse for Jane. One time, when Billy was on a three-day drug binge, he tied her to a chair when she came home from work. He ranted and raved at her all night with a shotgun in his hand, occasionally pointing the gun right at her. In the morning, after being up all night, Billy untied her and told her to go to work. The situation played out three nights in a row until Billy finally came down from his drug high.

Beyond the constant beatings Jane was subjected to, she suffered severe sexual abuse as well. Things got worse when Billy started working on the gypsum boats and going to ports in Europe and South America. His perversions became worse, as did his treatment of Jane. He always brought home a lot of pornographic magazines, sexy and degrading lingerie, perfumes and sex toys. Typically, when Billy came home, he showed Darren a gift that he had brought back for him, but wouldn't allow the boy to touch it. He then beat Darren and sent him to bed. Next, he tied Jane to a chair, legs splayed, and pulled out each individual pubic hair so that, he said, no other man would want her. That done, he checked Jane for any marks on her body, which she would have to explain, all the while calling her dirty names. He made her take a bath, and then covered her in the perfume he had bought. She would be forced to undress Billy while he pinched and poked her. From there, the ritual varied, but usually involved Jane being tied to the bed and beaten in some manner. He sometimes tied her spread-eagle and forced himself into her or sodomized her. The first few times he sodomized Jane, Billy complained that she was hurting him. He went outside and returned with a piece of two-centimetre plumbing pipe, 10 centimetres long, that he lubricated and forced into Jane's rectum. From then on, she had to keep the pipe in her whenever he was home and could only take it out when he wanted to sodomize her. Billy would also force Jane to masturbate in front of him, perform despicable acts with the family dog and drink Billy's urine—all while Billy intermittently beat her, shotgun close at hand.

Jane often contemplated suicide. Only thoughts of Darren kept her from doing so. "My son was the only thing that kept me from death and from losing my sanity. He was my strength, my gift from God, my whole instinct to survive." She also considered killing Billy while he slept, but was afraid that the mess Darren would see would be too much for the child. She thought about leaving, but knew Billy would follow through on his promise to kill her whole family. She seriously thought about going to the police. There was a spousal abuse case before the courts in a nearby town in which the wife had ended up hospitalized because of her husband, and Jane made the trip to watch the proceedings. The abuser only got a $200 fine and a peace bond against him. She knew that if she were in the same situation, Billy would kill her. She couldn't bear the thought of leaving Darren in that situation. She finally decided to try to hire someone to kill Billy.

Beverly Taylor, an acquaintance of Billy's, was also into drugs. Jane had overheard him talking about drug deals with Billy, and she thought he might be able to help her. Jane approached Taylor about killing Billy, offering him Billy's $20,000 life insurance policy as payment. Taylor declined. He suggested setting Billy up in a drug bust, but Jane knew that her husband would blame her, Allen or their boarder Ronny. Jane contacted Taylor a few more times, begging for help, but he always declined her offer.

BILLY'S LAST DAY: MARCH 11, 1982

Billy wanted to build a pigpen. The pigpen, he decided, would go between his home and Margaret Joudrey's. Margaret was furious. She thought that the pigpen would stink. They argued back and forth over whether or not Margaret owned her land.

When Billy and Jane were forced out of their first house, Margaret and Stanley Joudrey, a common-law couple, offered to give them a small piece of the Joudrey land for just the cost of the surveying and fees. So Billy bought a small trailer and put it on the property, making the Staffords and Joudreys neighbours. Then Stanley died. Because he did not have a will and Margaret was not legally his wife, she did not officially have title to the land—a fact that Billy often threw in her face. When Billy put the foundation for the pigpen over his property line, Margaret objected. Billy laughed at her and told her that she couldn't contest it, since she didn't own the land. Margaret screamed obscenities at Billy, all in front of Margaret's friend Roger Manthorne. Billy finally left the Joudrey's trailer but not before threatening to burn Margaret out.

Billy gathered up Allen and Ronny Wamboldt, and they left in the truck to pick up a load of sawdust for the pen. The men worked until midmorning, and Jane spent that time doing laundry and hanging it on the clothesline. Billy came in for lunch and a cup of tea, then went to the bedroom for a nap. Soon he was calling Jane in.

"Shut the door and strip. I want to screw you."

Jane did as she was told. Noticing the bruises on her body, she thought back to the brutal beating from days before, when Billy had beaten her with the metal hose from the vacuum cleaner. Climbing into bed, she prayed it would be over quickly. It was, and soon Billy was asleep. Jane got dressed and went back outside to bring in the laundry. She was ironing when Margaret Joudrey showed up at the door wanting to talk to Billy. The neighbour went straight into the bedroom and woke him up. She was still angry that Billy had talked about the land in front of Roger Manthorne, Margaret's new live-in boyfriend, and told Billy that she was going to fight him on it. "And I called the police and reported you for shooting at my trailer, and they're investigating it."

Billy flew into a rage. He threw Margaret out of the trailer. "You'd better have a good day, you old c***, because you'll never live to see another one." Billy's eyes were bulging, spit flying from his mouth, his face flushed. Jane knew she was in trouble. Billy demanded that Jane give him some money so he could go to town. When Jane told him she couldn't, he grabbed her laundry, took it outside and threw it into the mud. He took the clothes back in, slapped Jane around and then spat on her. Then Billy grabbed her purse, took all her money and left.

Ronny and Billy spent the whole afternoon drinking rum and smoking marijuana. By the time they returned for dinner, they were both intoxicated, but kept on drinking. Later in the evening, Billy made Jane drive him and Ronny to another friend's house, where they smoked more pot and drank even more. On the drive home, Billy, sitting in the middle, was raving about Margaret Joudrey.

"When Margaret turns her light off down there tonight, it'll be lights off for her, for good!... I'm going to dump [gasoline] all around that f***ing trailer and watch them burn." He suddenly looked Jane right in the eye and said, "And I'll deal with that son of yours at the same time. I've waited a long time to deal with him. I might as well clean them all up at one time." Billy laughed and laughed.

By the time Jane arrived home with Billy and Ronny, the men had fallen into a drunken stupor. Ronny stumbled from the truck and into his shack, while Billy slept soundly in the passenger seat. Allen was inside the house and had woken when he heard the truck pull up. Because Jane would always get a severe beating if she got out of the truck before Billy, she just sat behind the wheel and waited. "I just sat there and the words… everything that he had been saying, just started sinking in… Margaret…Allen. What was he going to do? I just said, 'To hell with it, I'm not going to live like this anymore.'"

Jane started honking the horn. Allen ignored it at first, but he eventually came outside to see what was going on. Jane asked him to get a gun and load it. He brought out a 12-gauge shotgun. Jane was standing beside the truck. She took the gun and told Allen to go back inside. Then Jane put the barrel through the open driver's side window and pulled the trigger.

Inside the house, Allen heard the shot, waited half a minute, and then went outside. Jane handed him the shotgun, then asked him to put some clean clothes in a garbage bag and bring them to her. When he came back, she said, "Take the gun down to Margaret's. Roger will help you get rid of it. And call your grandfather and tell him to meet me down by the satellite station." Jane then left the house and drove around for a while with Billy leaning against her. Finally, she ended up at the satellite station. She backed up as far as she could and got out of the truck, leaving the keys in the ignition. She did not know if Billy was dead or alive.

Allen ran down to Margaret's trailer. When Roger opened the door, Allen laid the gun down on the step and said, "Ma did it. I've got to use the phone." He called his grandparents. When Gladys answered, Allen told her to pick Jane up at the satellite station. Roger and Allen broke down the gun, walked down to the river just behind the property and threw the pieces off the bridge. Then they cleaned up the spots of blood outside the Stafford home.

Jane's parents picked her up. They asked her what was going on, but she wouldn't tell them. She just asked to go to their home so she could get cleaned up. At the Hurshman residence, Jane showered and changed into the clean clothes Allen had given her. She put the bloody clothes into the garbage bag. Her parents drove her home, but stopped just short of the house. Jane got out of the vehicle and walked through the bushes the rest of the way so no one would see her. When she got inside, she flashed the lights in the house to let Margaret Joudrey know she needed to talk to her. Margaret, Roger and Allen came straight over. Margaret hugged Jane and assured her that everything would be okay. Allen took the garbage bag of bloody clothes and burned them in the wood stove. Eventually, everyone went to bed, and it wasn't until the next day, when the police arrived at Jane's door, that she was sure Billy, her common-law husband of six years, was dead.

FINDING BILLY

The Teleglobe Satellite Station was one of the only places in the area to get a job. Walking to work at the station, Carl Croft noticed a Jeep truck parked off the side of the road. He didn't give it much attention until he saw the blood. "I got close to the truck, and I see there's blood all over the door, and I looked around the highway. I thought someone must have had an accident or something, but there was nothing tore up nowhere."

Investigating closer, Croft saw the body. "I looked at him, and I knowed he wasn't all there. I know he wasn't living." He ran to the home of his neighbour, John Babin. John was certified in first aid, so when Croft came to the door babbling about an accident, he thought he could help. The two men drove down to the truck, and Croft stayed in the vehicle while Babin checked out the situation. He knew immediately that the man was dead. Babin's son had committed suicide eight months prior, and that was the first thing that popped into his head. They returned to Babin's home and called the police.

When the police arrived, Babin told them there was a body in the truck—and it didn't have a head. The investigation quickly revealed that the head had been blown off the body by a shotgun blast, and there was particle matter all over the cab of the truck. Running a check on the licence plate showed that the truck belonged to Billy Stafford. Since he was well known to local police, one officer knew immediately it was Billy's body in the cab of the truck. The body's size was right, and the clothes were the same ones Billy had been wearing three days earlier when the officer pulled him over. The police also knew that Billy had a lot of enemies. Anyone could be a suspect.

Police drove to the Stafford house, stopping along the way at homes to see if anyone had noticed something strange the night before. No one had. When they arrived at the Stafford's property, Jane was just coming out of the Joudrey trailer. They asked her when she had seen Billy last, and she told them she hadn't seen him since he had left in the truck the night before. After making sure that the clothes on the body matched the clothes Billy had been wearing, RCMP Officer Pike said, "I'm sorry to inform you, we found your husband deceased in his truck this morning." Jane Stafford fainted.

THE INVESTIGATION

Jane became a suspect almost immediately. Police had heard rumours of her trying to hire a hit man, and they knew of Billy's penchant for beating his wife. Jane was in shock and disoriented when the police interviewed her, but she told them that Billy was heavily involved in drugs and suggested the mafia had killed him.

A few days later, police interviewed Beverly Taylor. He told them about Jane trying to hire him to kill Billy. It was enough to get a search warrant. In the days between the shooting and the search warrant, Jane had gone to the doctor and was given a prescription for Valium. She used it to get through those first days, and she had taken quite a few pills by the time the police came by on the evening of March 13. Constable McKnight took Jane to the station for questioning while officers searched her home.

The police interrogated Jane throughout the night, but she never veered from her original mafia story. Jane kept asking to speak to Lamont Stafford, and the police continually denied her request. They told her that they knew she had tried to hire Taylor to kill her husband, yet she stuck to her story. Finally, at 9:15 the next morning, after about eight hours of interrogation, Jane was allowed out of the small room. Her father, Maurice, and Billy's father, Lamont, were waiting for her.

Jane met with Lamont privately in a small room. She wanted to tell him face to face that she had killed his son. Jane felt it was important for him to know before anyone else. She then had a few minutes with her father before Staff Sergeant Williamson came in to question Jane again. "Did you kill Bill?" he asked. "Yes," Jane replied simply. Jane told the whole story—the abuse, the degradation, everything. Williamson cautioned her and had her repeat her story for a statement. For some reason, he did not include the details of the abuse. After taking the confession, Williamson talked to some officers. "She deserves a medal. She probably saved a couple of our officers' lives."

Jane was finally allowed to go home. She went straight to bed. Darren came into her bedroom. "Your father is dead. I killed him. He won't be coming home anymore." Darren asked her if that meant Billy wouldn't hurt them anymore. "He's gone forever," Jane told him. "I'm glad, Mommy," Darren said, hugging Jane tightly.

Justice For Whom?

Jane was charged with first-degree murder on March 16, five days after Billy's death. Jane retained lawyer Alan Ferrier, a legal aid lawyer, for her case. He had her see a psychiatrist and agreed to take her case. On June 7, Jane was committed to stand trial. She tried to plead guilty to manslaughter, but the Crown rejected her plea, stating that because Billy was asleep when he was shot, there was no apparent danger to Jane at that time. Because of that, the crime was classified as first-degree murder.

The trial began on November 2. In court, Ferrier argued against allowing Jane's confession because Staff Sergeant Williamson had not properly documented the history of abuse. The judge agreed, so the jury would never hear the statement. However, following a polygraph administered by the RCMP, Jane had given another statement. This one was ruled as admissible.

The prosecution presented Beverly Taylor to the jury. Taylor told the story of how Jane had tried to hire him to kill Billy. Then Ronny Wamboldt took the stand. The prosecution was trying to show Billy's nice side—that he had let Ronny live on his property when he had nowhere else to go. However, Wamboldt turned into a great defence witness when he recounted Billy's horrific abuse of both Darren and Jane. He told of the constant beatings that Darren suffered as a toddler and small boy as well as the force-feeding incidents. He told of the times Jane played cards with him and Billy. If Jane played a card that Billy didn't like, he would hit her so hard she would fall off the chair. She would get up, sit back down and keep on playing. When asked why Jane never stood up to Billy, Wamboldt told the court that if she had, "She would get it again."

Then Jane's son Allen took the stand. The prosecution led him through testimony regarding the gun. He also testified to the constant fighting between Margaret Joudrey and Billy. He said that Billy had threatened her more than once and that Margaret kept a loaded gun in their house in case Billy ever came in. Allen testified that he had asked Margaret about the gun, and she said, "If that fool ever comes down here causing trouble, he won't be walking back."

Roger Manthorne was called to the witness stand. He also testified to his actions with the gun on the night of the murder. He spoke to the fact that Margaret had comforted Jane that night and described the fight that Billy and Margaret had the day of Billy's death. He stated that Margaret was very upset by Billy's threats.

Margaret, on the other hand, turned against Jane in the trial, leaving Jane dumbfounded by her friend's testimony. Margaret stated that she and Billy had a "little argument" over the pigs. She admitted to arguing with Billy over the years, but denied that she was afraid of him—their quarrels were more like banter. Then the shock came. Margaret testified that it was Jane who had beaten Darren with the broomstick the day they went for a drive, and it was she who often beat Darren. She testified that she had never seen Billy raise a hand to his wife or child or any bruises on Jane.

Jane was horrified. Numerous times over the past years, Margaret had sat at the kitchen table while Billy had beaten both her and Darren. Her neighbour had been a witness to the abuse on more occasions than Jane could count. The cross-examination by Alan Ferrier was ugly. Repeatedly, the judge had to instruct Margaret to answer the questions. Ferrier forced her to admit that everyone else must be lying if she were telling the truth. He asked her why her feelings towards Jane had suddenly changed. Margaret replied, "Because she got me mixed up in this, and there is no need of it." Jane believes that Margaret was angry at having it come out that she didn't have lawful title to her land. The pain of having the woman who was her closest friend lie about the abuse she had suffered was palpable.

Jane's mother Gladys took the stand and testified that Jane and her parents did not have a close relationship. She said that after Billy had beaten up Maurice and damaged the Hurshman home, the Hurshmans did not see a lot of Jane and Billy.

Police officers took the stand and testified about the bruises on Jane's body when she was arrested, the search of the house and Jane's interrogation. They said that Billy was well known by the police for his violence and volatile personality. They admitted that many officers were afraid of Billy Stafford. Billy's rap sheet, three pages long, was introduced as evidence, as was the statement made by Staff Sergeant Williamson that Jane deserved a medal.

Next, Jane's statement was read to the court:

Question: What can you tell me about Billy Stafford's death on March the 11th, '82?

Answer: I killed him.

Question: Where and how did it happen?

Answer: In the truck in our yard in Bangs Falls. We arrived home, and Ronny went in and went to bed. I just sat in the truck because Bill was asleep or passed out or something. I waited a little while, I don't know how long, maybe 20 minutes or half an hour. I beeped the horn a couple of times, and Al came to the door. I just told him to get me the gun and load it. He came back out with the gun, and by that time, I had gotten out of the truck. I got the gun from Al, and he went back inside. I just laid the gun over the driver's window and pulled the trigger. It was just a big mess.

The prosecution rested.

Jane was terrified to take the stand. All she could think about was what she would do if they showed her pictures of Billy's body. She had not known that Billy's head had been blown off when she shot him, and she was afraid she wouldn't be able to handle seeing the pictures in court. Luckily, the prosecution never showed her the photos.

Jane took the stand on November 16, 1982. She spoke so quietly throughout her testimony that the judge had to ask her repeatedly to speak up. Alan Ferrier led Jane through her story. She described her early life with her parents, her brief marriage and the suffering she and her children had endured at the hands of Billy Stafford. Ferrier asked why she didn't leave. She told the court about the threats Billy had made that he would kill her family. She continued the next day, testifying about the horrors of simple family activities such as having dinner and how the beatings just got worse and worse. She told the court about Billy selling drugs and the abuse she suffered while he was high.

Ferrier asked Jane about Margaret Joudrey. She told the court that Margaret was like a mother to her and knew everything that went on in the Stafford home. When Ferrier asked why Jane killed Billy when she did, she described how he had raved about burning out Margaret and his intention to kill Allen. She testified that Billy had admitting to killing Jimmy LeBlanc on the fishing boat years earlier and told the court about his threats to kill others in the community. By the time she stepped down, she was exhausted but relieved.

Three psychiatrists took the stand next. They testified that Jane was depressed and had low self-esteem. She was emotionally immature and lacked proper planning capability. They stated that she had been under overwhelming emotional stress for years. In their opinion, Billy's murder could not have been a well-thought-out plan, but was more of an emotional reaction to her horrible situation—she had been living on the defensive against Billy for years.

Neighbours and people from the community all testified on Jane's behalf. They described various situations in which Billy had attacked or threatened people in the community, and told the court about Billy's violent nature. Others testified to witnessing the abuse Jane suffered. The defence rested its case on evidence given by Pauline, Billy's first wife. She described the abuse she and her children had been subjected to while married to Billy. By the time the defence wrapped up its case, it was obvious that Margaret Joudrey had lied on the stand.

The prosecution put forth its case that Jane be found guilty of first-degree murder because, since Billy was asleep, Jane had not been defending herself against an active threat. Ferrier argued that the constant abuse Jane faced and the imminent threats to both Margaret Joudrey and Jane's son Allen were enough to have Jane found not guilty. The judge charged the jury, and they began their deliberations at 5:30 PM on November 19 and had made a decision by 11:00 AM on November 20. The courtroom was silent as the judge asked for their verdict.

"Not guilty," the jury foreman responded.

The courtroom erupted.

Women's groups across Canada called the jury's decision a victory for all women. Other individuals argued that Jane should have gone to prison—she had killed a man, after all—and predicted that there would be an increase in vigilantism. Alan Ferrier believes that the jury could not ignore the severe abuse that Darren had suffered. Some thought that Jane could have left, but Darren was innocent and unable to protect himself. Ferrier thinks that is why Jane was forgiven.

The prosecution was not happy. They appealed Jane's conviction and won the right to another trial. However, understanding that the odds of winning were not in their favour, the Crown accepted a plea of guilty to manslaughter from Jane, who did not want the ordeal of having to go to court again. At her sentencing hearing, Jane was given a six-month jail sentence and two years of probation. She was also allowed to attend classes to complete the nursing assistant's course that she had been working at since Billy's death. Jane was satisfied with the verdict. She served one-third of her sentence, and on April 14, 1984, walked out of prison. She completed her parole and probation and was a free woman, at least legally, on August 14, 1986.

Finding Jane

Jane changed her name back to Hurshman, moved to Halifax and worked at a care facility as a nursing assistant for several years. She fought tirelessly to protect other women from abuse. She became famous, especially after a 1984 interview on CBC's *Fifth Estate*. When Jane recounted her horrors, the interview had to be stopped because the microphones were picking up the sound of her panicked heart over top of her voice. In 1986, Brian Vallée wrote a book called *Life With Billy* that detailed Jane's story and was a major resource for this piece. The book was a bestseller in Canada.

Jane remarried and lived with her boys in Halifax. She received both accolades and death threats, and the pressure of being Jane Stafford never ceased. She shot herself in the chest in her car on the Halifax waterfront in February 1992.

~

Chapter Eight

Cheryl Capistrano

A man is unconscious on the sofa when the police come in. They can quickly tell he is gravely injured. Blood is seeping from massive wounds to his head and is spattered everywhere. Part of his ear is missing. Police try to wake him. Moans of agony. The ambulance arrives quickly and whisks the man away. Six days later, he is dead. The media quickly label his next-door neighbour the "Barbeque Killer." ∾

THE OFFICIAL VERSION

An hour north of the United States–Canada border lies the city of Winnipeg, Manitoba. Although fewer than 650,000 people call Winnipeg home, it is the capital of this central Canadian province. Winnipeg is known for its harsh winters—the cold descends in late October and doesn't lift until well into spring. But the summers are hot, and the grass and flowers are abundant. Winnipeg touts itself as being family friendly, with parks in all areas of the city, family activities, festivals and the zoo. But in 1997, the downtown core of the city was rife with the homelessness that affects many North American cities—panhandlers, windshield washers and drunks. And just outside the downtown, near the railyards, lies Alexander Avenue. Closely built homes and apartments line the old street. This inner-city area has the highest homicide and sexual assault rates in the city. Violence is commonplace, as is drunkenness and drug use. It's the kind of area where no one should be out after dark.

It was August 30, 1997. Near the end of an unusually hot summer, the warm evening seemed like the perfect night for a barbeque. Carl Trotter went next door to his neighbours' apartment to invite them over. Cheryl Capistrano answered the door. Trotter invited Capistrano and her live-in boyfriend, Jack Lowry, to bring their hibachi over to his backyard. Carl would supply the beer, and they could all enjoy the night. Cheryl had only met Carl once before, but she was always up for a party. The couple headed next door after convincing their good friends Sheree Kaminski and Lucien "Tongue" McKenzie to join them. When they arrived, Carl and his wife, as well as another neighbour, Judy Smith, were in the yard. Cheryl had known Judy most of her life. She felt immediately comfortable as the party began.

According to court documents, it was pretty late when the party got started. Jack, already quite drunk, decided to head home and straight to bed fairly soon after arriving. Everyone else kept going. The mood was light-hearted and fun, casual talk among neighbours—Blue Bombers not doing well that year, too many mosquitoes—small talk. But as the evening turned into night and the drinking got heavier, Carl started being obnoxious. He laughed while everyone else, drunk as well, became offended. Cheryl decided it was time for the party to move to her own yard. Carl was not welcome, but Cheryl invited his wife to come. Trotter could be heard as the group walked away, calling Capistrano a bitch that wouldn't be invited back.

Carl, not happy about being left alone, soon staggered into the backyard of Cheryl's apartment building. She was just coming down the stairs from her apartment. "I like the way your tits bounce when you walk down the stairs," Carl leered. Tongue McKenzie jumped out of his chair. "Don't f-in' talk to her that way!" He tried to get Carl to apologize. Trotter, drunk, refused, and the two men fought. Tongue came out decidedly on top, and Carl skulked back to his own yard. He came back minutes later with a pipe wrench and swung it at Cheryl. Again, Tongue jumped in. The pair wrestled, and Carl ended up on the ground. He stayed down for a short period of time, and then stumbled back to his own house. Cheryl went upstairs and got a Louisville Slugger baseball bat in case he came back.

Carl, never one to quit, went to the end of the fence that divided the properties and started calling out to the group. Cheryl picked up her bat and went to the fence. "You want some more? Some more?" she shouted at him. Carl quickly backed away from the fence and, according to the official version of the story, went into his house. The group, deciding that he was too much trouble, moved their gathering into Judy Smith's home two doors down.

While at the party, Cheryl approached her friend Sheree Kaminski. She told Kaminski that she had hit Carl earlier and wanted to check on him. Although Sheree couldn't remember seeing Cheryl leave earlier, she agreed to accompany her friend.

When they got to Carl's home, it was completely dark. Cheryl flicked on the light, saw Carl passed out on the sofa and switched the light off again. Sheree heard Carl breathing and said, "See, he's fine." The pair left and went back to Judy's house.

Eventually, the party ended, and everyone returned to their respective homes. It wasn't until the next morning that police got a call from Judy Smith stating that Carl Trotter had been injured. When the police arrived, Carl was unconscious on the sofa in the living room. He was covered in blood and had massive head injuries. Part of his ear was missing. He woke up soon after the police arrived and began to moan in pain. The police called an ambulance, something Carl's wife had failed to do. She told police that she had not seen anything and didn't know her husband was injured until she got up in the morning. Because she had been partying with the neighbours, she could not provide the police with any information at all. She did tell them that Cheryl had fought with Carl the night before, so the police headed next door to talk to Capistrano.

Police knocked on the door of 1294 Alexander Avenue at 9:00 AM on August 31, 1997. Cheryl answered the door. Constable Legge of the Winnipeg Police Service told her about Trotter's injuries. He then asked her about the fight she had with Trotter. She told the police that she had taken a bat out to the yard to protect herself because of the incident with the pipe wrench. Cheryl's boyfriend, Jack Lowry, brought the bat to the officer and handed it over. When another officer, Constable Dudek, told Cheryl she was a suspect, she said, "Me? No way, man. If anything, I should be charging him. He came at me with that wrench." She pointed to the pipe wrench lying in the backyard.

Constable Dudek asked Cheryl to come to the police station "to clear things up," and she agreed to go. The officer escorted her to the police cruiser and went back for the pipe wrench. Following procedure, Dudek placed the wrench, which had two smears and a strand of hair stuck to it, into a plastic evidence bag and put the bag in the trunk of the cruiser.

Cheryl was taken to a police station holding room, where she was questioned about her neighbour's vicious beating. Repeatedly, she denied hitting Carl Trotter and told the police that she had seen him asleep on the couch, totally drunk but alive late the night before.

On September 5, 1997, Trotter died from his injuries. Cheryl Capistrano was arrested and charged with second-degree murder.

Before the trial could begin in 2000, almost three years after Trotter's death, the judge had to rule on an application made by the defence. The defence argued that the charges against their client should be dropped because the police had lost the evidence. Apparently, after placing Capistrano in a cell, Constable Dudek handed the pipe wrench to another officer. Sometime during the transfer of evidence, the hair on the pipe wrench was lost. The defence felt that they could not mount a proper case if important, possibly exculpatory evidence was missing. Court of Queen's Bench Justice Hanssen agreed. "The strand of hair on the wrench was lost as a result of unacceptable negligence on the part of the police." However, he felt that the loss of the evidence would have no bearing on the overall outcome of the case.

The trial was held in the spring of 2001, and, in the end, a jury found Cheryl guilty of Carl's murder. On March 1, 2001, Cheryl Capistrano was given a conditional sentence of two years less a day to be served in her home. She had strict conditions put on her, but she was able to live in the community. Taking Capistrano's difficult life circumstances into account, Justice Hanssen concluded his sentencing by stating:

> "The sentence being imposed on Ms. Capistrano is
> not a lenient one. While she is being allowed to

serve her sentence in the community, her liberty will be severely restricted. In effect, she is being imprisoned in her home rather than in an institution. Except as otherwise permitted under the terms of the conditional sentence order, she will be confined to her home for the next two years less a day... The police and her supervisor will be doing random checks on her. If she is not at home when she is supposed to be there, or if she breaches any of the other conditions of the conditional sentence order, she will be arrested. If this occurs, it would likely mean that she would be required to serve the balance of her sentence in a prison."

Cheryl's Story

Cheryl Capistrano was born on October 14, 1968. She did not have a happy childhood. By the age of 12, Cheryl was the victim of sexual abuse by her father, Donald Lafreniere. According to Cheryl, he was an alcoholic and politically connected. He worked as a representative for the NDP government in Manitoba as well as for the Department of Indian Affairs. His work took him all over the world and into many hotel rooms, where he abused his daughter. Cheryl lived through years of serious emotional, physical and sexual abuse. When she was 12, the Children's Aid Society took her into their care. She was admitted to the Merrymount Institution, illegally according to Cheryl, without any formal psychological evaluation. She lived there for seven and a half years. While locked up in the institution, Cheryl tried to commit suicide numerous times. Looking back, she thinks that the government covered up her father's crimes against her because of his high government position.

At 19, Cheryl got married. Her husband was abusive towards her and was also a criminal. Eventually, he was deported from Canada, and Cheryl and her two children from the marriage were free. However, she was not able to care for them properly, and they were taken away by Children's Aid. Once they were out of her care permanently, they were adopted, and she was allowed no contact whatsoever with them.

Cheryl became addicted to drugs and followed in her father's footsteps to become an alcoholic. In her 20s, Cheryl was violently raped by a stranger, and the incident triggered a severe case of post-traumatic stress disorder.

She also had various run-ins with the law in her 20s and was convicted of assault, possession of a weapon and obstructing a police officer. In 1997, Cheryl was just starting to get her life in order. She had met a great man, Jack Lowry, who was helping her with her problems, and they had a nice apartment. Although she lived in the inner city, Cheryl considered the area to be "quite good." She had a job working as a maid in a hotel, and things seemed to be getting better for her. Then she met Carl Trotter.

Cheryl admits that she and her friends went over to the Trotters' backyard that night. She agrees that Carl Trotter invited them. However, almost immediately, her story differs from that of the official court documents. Cheryl says that soon after her boyfriend Jack went to bed, Carl started being abusive to his wife. At first it was just verbal, but then he started pushing her around. Cheryl said to her friends that they should move to her yard. They invited Carl's wife to join them but told Carl there was no way he was allowed. This is what caused Trotter to call Capistrano a bitch.

Cheryl, Sheree, Judy, Carl's wife and Tongue all went next door to Capistrano's. After the first altercation between Tongue and Carl, Cheryl remembers sitting in a chair with her back to the entrance of the yard. All of a sudden, Tongue leapt out of his chair and directly at Cheryl. She thought he was going to attack her, but he continued past her and took two swings at Carl. Tongue had seen Carl sneak up behind Capistrano and raise a pipe wrench above her head to strike a violent blow. After Tongue and Carl wrestled over the pipe wrench, Trotter went back home.

At this point, Carl's wife and Judy Smith told Cheryl that they thought Carl was going to kill her and that she wasn't safe. Looking back, she felt they were trying to rile her up and pit her against Carl. Cheryl went upstairs and grabbed the Louisville Slugger baseball bat, "the real light kind," she stated. She said she was scared of Carl at that point because she had only just met him, and two women who knew him were telling her she was in danger. When Carl appeared at the fence, he started swearing at his wife and threatening her. Cheryl jumped up and told him to leave his wife and the rest of them alone or she would call the cops. She picked up the bat and told him that if he came back, she would "give him some more." Carl's wife and Judy Smith told Cheryl that they thought she was in big trouble with Trotter. They wanted to move the party to Judy's house two doors down. The group agreed, so the party moved again.

Everything was good at Smith's house, but Cheryl was really angry with Carl. She didn't like being pushed out of her own yard because she was trying to protect someone else. She approached Sheree.

"Come with me. I'm going to go talk to him, tell him he can't push me around."

"No way, let it go. He's drunk is all," Sheree told her.

Cheryl says that she really wanted to confront Carl, and the only way to get Sheree to come with her was to lie.

"I hit him in the head. I just want to make sure he's okay."

"No ya didn't, Cherie. You were here the whole time."

"Really! Come on. Just come check."

Sheree agreed to go with her friend even though she knew that Cheryl hadn't left the party at all since they arrived.

When the two women got to the Trotters' house, it was pitch dark. Sheree stayed at the door when Cheryl turned on the light. Sheree said that she could hear Carl breathing. Cheryl said that when the light came on, she saw Carl lying passed out on the sofa. He was breathing, and there was no blood anywhere in the room. Sheree said, "See Cher, no problem. He's fine." Cheryl switched off the light, closed the door and never saw Carl again.

The pair went back to the party and hung out a bit longer. Soon though, everyone was tired, and Cheryl and her friends went home. She believes that Carl's wife left at some point after that.

In court, the Crown argued that Cheryl must have gone back to Trotter's home at some point after the party and killed him. They introduced blood spatter evidence that showed a massive struggle. According to Jack Lowry, there was "blood all over that place," yet the baseball bat did not have a single drop of blood on it. Being that Carl Trotter was over 180 centimetres tall and "kinda beefy, like a heavy drinker," Cheryl would have been at the wrong end of a fight with him. At the time, she weighed barely 48 kilograms, was still suffering from a bad car accident, and is only about 150 centimetres tall. The police never found any evidence of blood in Capistrano's home or on her clothes. She had no marks or scratches that would indicate that she had been in a fight—but someone else did. And even today, this is where Cheryl gets really upset. She feels that the police refused to investigate further or suspect anyone other than herself. Had they, she feels, the police would agree with what she thinks happened that night.

Cheryl believes that Trotter's wife, tired of being abused by her spouse, hired Judy Smith to kill Carl Trotter. It was Judy who called the police the morning that Carl was found injured. Smith had a badly battered face the day after the party. When Cheryl asked Judy what happened, Smith told her she had fallen down some stairs. Cheryl thinks that the friends saw their chance when Carl got into an argument with Tongue, and Cheryl brought down the bat. She remembers them pushing to move the party and scaring her into thinking that Carl would come after her. She believes the pair framed her and even pointed police firmly in her direction. Soon after Carl's death, Judy had a sudden influx of money. When asked about it, she was extremely vague, though at one point, she claimed that she had inherited it. Cheryl believes that Carl's wife paid Judy for killing her husband that night. In her testimony in court, Capistrano raised all these points, but the jury didn't buy it. They found her guilty of second-degree murder anyway.

Cheryl feels that the judge and the Crown prosecutor actually believed her side of the story. She thinks that is why she got the "light" sentence of two years less a day. She had to complete her community service requirements, but police never checked on her, and she never had to report to a court-appointed supervisor after her initial meeting. She also says that the Crown prosecutor approached her after the court sentencing and told her that if she didn't appeal her conviction or speak out in public during her sentence as to what she believes truly happened, the Crown wouldn't appeal the sentence or have her incarcerated. Cheryl believes that was why there was such a low level of surveillance on her during her two-year sentence.

Cheryl Capistrano completed her sentence and now lives in a good neighbourhood in Winnipeg with Jack Lowry. The pair got married in 2000. "We had to get married in the back-yard because of the sentence," she laughs. "There was no honey-moon!" She has her own housekeeping business and life is good for her. Recently, one of her sons who had been adopted out, now 20 years old, contacted her. Cheryl has kept all the newspaper clippings of both her father's trial and her own. She showed them all to her son and told him her whole story. "He doesn't care. He knows I didn't do it," she states plainly.

After the court case and her conditional sentence had been completed, Cheryl ran into Carl Trotter's wife on the street one day. Cheryl said to her, "I know you did it. It'll come back to you." Mrs. Trotter just turned and walked away.

~

Chapter Nine

Adele Gruenke

Vic Black pulled over to look at the Ford Tempo that was parked in the ditch. The windows were frosted over, and he couldn't see into the car. Squinting through the glass, he saw something in the front seat. He tapped on the window, but there was no response from inside the car. The car was locked, and the −8°C weather was not comfortable. Feeling cold and deciding that everything was fine, he drove off. River Road was not busy that night, and two hours passed before another person stopped. Robert Porteous also thought the lone Tempo was odd, sitting down in the ditch off an ice-free highway. He pulled up behind the car and shone his headlights in the rear window. It was still covered with frost, and he couldn't see anything. Porteous walked around the car until he found a gap in the frost. He was not prepared for the carnage inside. Frozen pieces of an old man's skull were all over the interior, and his body was slumped in the front seat. Quickly returning home, Porteous called the police. He did not know that his grisly discovery would eventually lead to the establishment of new parameters for confidentiality in the Canadian criminal justice system. ∽

I n 1985, 21-year-old Adele Gruenke began offering a new service in Winnipeg, Manitoba—reflexology. The almost unheard of treatment involved using pressure points on the foot to treat problem areas in the rest of the body. Because of its uniqueness, the *Winnipeg Sun* ran an article on the procedure and the therapist offering it. La Femme Total salon was offering the service in the ritzy area of River Heights.

Born and raised in Winnipeg, Adele was used to being in the spotlight. An attractive young woman, she loved being the centre of attention and, in her teens, often modelled for a well-known Pontiac dealership in town. Tall and brunette, she wanted to be Miss Park Pontiac, a coveted promotional position. She dated frequently during high school and was known for her bubbly personality.

Tragedy struck the Gruenke family when Michael, Adele's father, was diagnosed with leukemia. Tension in the family escalated and affected Adele in her late teens. Like many families dealing with cancer, life centred on going back and forth to the hospital. Michael's condition grew worse, and chemotherapy did not help. Adele found the five-year, torturous affair with modern medicine too much to bear. It seems she felt that she couldn't trust regular doctors and hospital care, which may have led her to the unusual practice of reflexology. Adele's father died when she was 20. He was 55.

Adele was still grieving for her father when she received a call at La Femme Total. An elderly gentleman contacted her after seeing the article about the reflexology sessions in the *Winnipeg Sun*. Adele explained the proactive methodology behind her sessions and booked an appointment for Mr. Philip Barnett.

Philip Barnett had also recently suffered a loss. His wife had died a month previously after a lifelong battle with alcoholism. The Barnetts lived in a modest apartment. Philip was constantly trying to keep the peace with the other tenants because his wife could be loud and obnoxious when drunk. There were frequent confrontations between husband and wife, and Philip's life was a constant balancing act. With no children, Philip suddenly found himself alone upon his wife's death.

Although he was 81, Philip could have been mistaken for a much younger man. He kept himself active by volunteering to clean the sidewalks around the building and always took the stairs to and from his third-floor apartment. He loved women and was known to be a flirt. He often propositioned the apartment manager, Kate Ford. He would give her little kisses on the cheek, hugs whenever he could sneak one, and would ask her to give him spankings. He was more pesky than threatening, and Kate would laugh him off and shoo him on his way.

Philip showed up for his appointment and told Adele that he was having trouble with his hip. During the reflexology session, the two commiserated over the losses they had recently both suffered. They immediately hit it off. Philip became a father figure to Adele, something she had been craving long before the strained relationship with her father had ended with his death. Adele was like the daughter that Philip never had.

Philip started having weekly reflexology sessions with Adele. He almost always showed up with a gift—chocolate, flowers, small tokens. After the sessions, the pair often went for coffee or lunch. They both found the situation mutually agreeable. Soon, the gifts became much more extravagant. Philip sent Adele on at least two trips, one to Vancouver and one to Los Angeles. He bought her expensive clothing and jewellery, scuba gear and even a new car. He paid for a course for her at the University of Manitoba. Philip also began taking an avid interest in Adele's career. He gave her $1700 to start her own reflexology business within an affluent hair salon in Winnipeg. Adele accepted all of Philip's presents with open arms.

Eleven months later, Adele received $15,000 from her mother to use as a down payment on a home. Philip put up the rest of the money, and the two bought an $89,000 house in a prestigious part of the city. Joanna Gruenke, Adele's mother, was concerned about the relationship. Adele assured her that it was not intimate—she and Philip were simply friends. The pair spent a great deal of time together, eating out, going to movies or just staying in and watching TV.

Philip decided to get credit cards for Adele, as she was doing the grocery shopping for them. She bought a lot more than just food, but Barnett paid the bills happily. However, he soon felt that he should be getting more for his money than just a platonic companionship and started pressuring her to have sex with him. However, after agreeing to let him suck on her toes, she felt "awkward" and put a stop to it. Adele says that shortly after that, about a month after they moved in together, Philip stopped forwarding messages left by friends to her and would get jealous of any presents she received from other men. This did not stop Adele from applying to a school in Boulder, Colorado, for an expensive, 15-month course in naturopathic therapy, with the understanding that Philip would pay. She was accepted to the program and closed her business in the spring.

Shortly afterwards, Adele began to date Garth Davisson. She complained to him frequently about Philip's advances towards her and his pressure for "repayment" in a physical way. As spring led to summer, Adele started to lose a lot of weight and told Garth she thought she had leukemia, just like her father. Telling Philip she was too sick to continue living with him, she moved in with her mother. Philip was furious and told her that she wouldn't get away with walking out on him. They fought for a while, and then Adele called an old friend, James Fosty, to help her move out. Philip called her a few days later, full of apologies for what he had said, and begged her to come back to him. She told him she would never live with him again. Adele testified in court that she had grown afraid of Philip's constant sexual advances and jealous behaviour.

Alarmed by her weight loss, Adele and her boyfriend Garth went to Portland, Oregon, to a natural healing centre so she could be tested for leukemia. They found out she did not have cancer, but instead needed an intensive, and expensive, vitamin treatment. When Adele returned to Winnipeg in August 1986, she went straight to Philip. He immediately offered to pay Adele's $250-a-week vitamin costs. She apparently forgot her disgust at his advances, and the pair started to hang out again.

In October, Garth, fed up with Adele, broke up with her. Adele tried to cry on Philip's shoulder, but he flew into a rage. He apparently thought that Adele and Garth were just friends. Adele says that Philip told her, "If you can put out for Davisson, you can certainly put out for me. I have spent so much money and time on you, I should get something in return." Adele was shocked by Philip's words. "I thought of this person as someone who was helping me...I told him the more he persisted, the sicker I became. I would just think about this, and I would get myself really sick." However, Barnett kept trying.

On November 28, Philip decided that he'd had enough. Adele says that he set up a date with her, expecting to finally get repaid for the money he had given her. She called her old friend James Fosty, who tried to convince her not to go. Then the pair hatched a better plan.

Police found the body of Phil Barnett exactly where Robert Porteous had described. The Ford Tempo had been driven into the ditch purposefully, judging by the tire tracks.

There was blood everywhere, and skull fragments were found all over the front seat and as far down as the gas pedal. Barnett's money and identification were still in his wallet, so the police quickly ruled out theft as a motive. The chief medical examiner, Dr. Peter Markesteyn, concluded that Barnett had died as a result of blunt-force trauma.

When the police searched Philip's house, they found it clean and orderly. Oddly, they also found Barnett's will lying conspicuously on top of his dresser in the bedroom. The will, dated four months earlier, left everything to Adele Gruenke.

Three kilometres from the car was a small farmhouse. The owner of the house called the police because she had found a toque and seen blood-soaked snow in her driveway. Officers soon discovered hair, a human tooth and part of a pair of glasses in the area as well.

Investigators went to see Adele. When they told her that Philip was dead, she simply asked them if they knew how he had died. Sergeant Bell of the Winnipeg Police asked Adele if she would come to the station to answer some questions. During the interrogation, she spoke freely about her relationship with Barnett and the large amounts of money he spent on her. She told them about the clothes, the money for the vitamins, the money for her business, the trips and the car. "Why would I want to kill someone who paid all my bills?" she asked the officers.

James Fosty was also at the station. James told police that he and Adele had spent the day shopping and visiting friends. Then they went to their respective homes to change for a night out and got back together in the evening. They cleaned Fosty's car, had a bite to eat and played pool. He said they were together all night. In Adele's five-page statement, she reiterated the same series of events.

Police needed to poke holes in the pair's story. One of the places that James and Adele had gone on November 28, the day of the murder, was the Nor-Villa Hotel. While they were there, a carpenter in the building had asked Fosty to sell him a nail puller, and Fosty returned that evening with the tool. When Winnipeg Police questioned the carpenter, they also took the nail puller into evidence. It had blood on the handle.

Officers also searched Adele's mother's home, where they found little beyond an outdated will of Barnett's. This will named Adele as the executor as well as the sole beneficiary. Her possession of the document cemented police's suspicions that Adele had killed the old man for his money.

Then investigators paid a visit to James Fosty. When they arrived, Fosty welcomed the officers into his home, taking their jackets and offering them a drink. He was cordial and jovial. Police asked to search his car, and Fosty offered to drive it to the station. Instead, they took him to the station in a squad car. Like Adele, James talked the whole ride. However, this time the conversation had nothing to do with the case. When they arrived at the station, James spoke to his lawyer and quickly decided to remain silent.

After questioning all the suspects in the case, the police decided that the pair killed Barnett in the driveway of the farmhouse, and then drove his car a few kilometres down the road and dumped it in the ditch. At the beginning of December 1986, Adele Gruenke and James Fosty were charged with murder and remanded to Winnipeg's Public Safety Building. The police took hair and blood samples from Adele. Prison was difficult for her, and she became suicidal in her cell, always sleeping right in the middle of the floor. In January, released on bail, Adele went to visit a counsellor she'd seen earlier in the year, Janine Frovich.

Frovich was a counsellor at a born-again Christian church, the Victorious Faith Centre. Near the end of September 1986, two months before the murder of Philip Barnett, she met Adele Gruenke. Adele had told Janine about her problems with Barnett. She said that she wanted a father-daughter relationship, but Barnett only wanted sex. Adele told the counsellor that she really needed the money he was giving her and was thinking of killing Philip for the money she would get from his estate. Frovich testified later in court that she "didn't take her [Adele] too seriously at the time." As the weeks passed, Janine regularly saw Adele at the church, even occasionally with Philip, and at the end of October, Adele told Janine that she no longer needed counselling. Frovich thought that her client had looked better in recent weeks—Adele had been afraid that she had leukemia when they first met—and Adele told Janine that things were better with Barnett and she no longer had thoughts of killing him. The counsellor felt "comfortable with that." However, when Garth Davisson broke up with Adele, she returned to Janine and told her that she was devastated. Not only that, now Barnett wanted sex again.

As soon as Janine heard the news that Philip Barnett had been killed, she thought of the threats Adele had made months earlier. Frovich told the court, "God did confirm an inner gut feeling that she had done it." She contacted Adele before the police had put the pieces together. Adele was upset, so Janine and her husband, Bill, went over to Adele's home. Adele did not feel comfortable, so the trio returned to the Frovich residence. Adele asked Bill and Janine if God could forgive someone who had committed murder. Frovich asked Adele what she was really trying to say, and Adele replied, "I killed Phil," and started crying.

The counsellor decided to call the pastor of the church, Harmony Thiessen. She explained the situation, and the pastor agreed to meet Janine and Adele at the church later that night. Adele was crying when the pastor came into his office that evening, and Janine was rubbing Adele's back to comfort her. Pastor Thiessen said, "Adele, you sure got yourself into a big one now."

Adele told the pastor about beating Philip and said that she had an alibi. She also said that she beat the old man because she was disgusted by his insistence on having sex. Adele was full of regret and said that if she had known how it would have gone and that she would end up getting caught, she wouldn't have done it. She told the pastor that she had planned the killing to look like a robbery but had forgotten to take Barnett's wallet. She felt that Philip had backed her into a corner by threatening to stop paying for her vitamin treatments—the only thing she considered to be keeping her alive—so she killed him.

Pastor Thiessen and Janine Frovich convinced Adele that she needed a lawyer and should talk to police. When she told James Fosty later that night, he was very upset. He told Adele that he hated her plan and should never have gotten involved.

Later, when Adele had been charged and released on bail, she went straight back to Janine Frovich. She begged the counsellor not to testify against her at the trial. Janine told Adele that she had no choice. She would stick by Adele, but would never lie.

The trial got underway on October 13, 1987. Fosty and Gruenke were tried together on charges of first-degree murder. The prosecutor, George Dangerfield, told the court that Adele, "tiring of these protestations that Barnett was making, an insistence that he have sex with her, elicited the help of Fosty and together went to Lorette [Manitoba] with Barnett. Together they killed him, together they took his body to where it was found some 13 kilometres away from where he was killed, and together they made up the story to cover up what they had done that particular night."

Officers testified about the scene where the body was found, the blood and skull fragments, and the blows to the back of Barnett's head and shoulder areas. Police found Barnett's blood in the wheel well of Fosty's car and on Fosty's clothes. RCMP Corporal Agnew testified that Barnett had written cheques to Adele totalling over $26,000, and she stood to inherit close to $250,000 from his estate. Beyond that were all the gifts and credit card purchases that Barnett had paid for over the year that the two had been "friends."

Janine Frovich took the stand, after much debate by defence counsel as to the admissibility of a confession made to a counsellor and pastor. The trial judge, Justice Ruth Krindle, ruled that Frovich's testimony was admissible because, among other things, the statements of the pastor and the counsellor had been allowed at the preliminary trial without objection and because confidentiality was not recognized as a tenet of that particular church. Frovich told the court about the confession that Adele made to her and recounted the conversations they had in her own living room with her husband present, at Adele's home and in the pastor's office. She also testified to the conversation between James and Adele in which Adele told him she was going to the police.

Adele took the stand in her own defence. She told the court that Philip had pushed her for sexual favours and that she couldn't take it anymore. Adele said that Philip had even threatened to hurt her mother if she did not comply. On the night of the murder, Barnett had apparently told her it was her last chance to "give it up to him" or else he would cut off the flow of money.

Frightened, Adele asked James to wait in his car while she talked to Philip, who was going over to her mother's home. As soon as she got into Philip's car, he took off. "He got right in about, you know, the two years that he had wasted, all of this money he had put into me, and he figured by spending all of this money that I would be grateful to him. That it wouldn't be that hard to convince me that I was doing him a big favour by engaging in sexual practices with him."

Adele tried to jump from the moving car, and the two struggled. Philip laughed at her, telling her that they were too far from town for anyone to hear her. Adele grabbed a "wooden handle that was on the floor in the passenger seat," struck Philip on the head and jumped out of the car. He chased her, and the pair wrestled on the ground. James, who had followed them, ran up. Adele recalled seeing his feet, but not much afterwards. The next thing she knew, Philip was covered in blood, and Adele became hysterical. James told her to drive the Tempo, and he would drive his own car. Adele testified that she thought they were going to a hospital to get help for Barnett, but instead they drove into a ditch. They cleaned off Fosty's car in a car-wash, and then went to a hotel. The two planned their story carefully and agreed never to implicate one another.

Dangerfield went at Adele hard. He made her admit to lying about having leukemia to Davisson and to constantly misleading the police. He reviewed the evidence about the large amounts of money Adele had received from Barnett and what she stood to inherit. He pushed her in an attempt to show that she was lying about the sexual advances of the older man just so she could kill him in "self-defence." Adele stuck to her story.

After a 10-day trial and five hours of deliberation, the jury returned a verdict of guilty of first-degree murder for both Adele Gruenke and James Fosty. They both automatically received sentences of life in prison with no chance of parole for 25 years.

However, Adele appealed her sentence. In her appeal, she argued that because of the nature of her relationship with her counsellor and pastor, they should not have been allowed to testify in court. The Court of Appeal of Manitoba decided that confession as a spiritual practice was not a tenet of the Victorious Faith Centre. In fact, the confession that Adele had made to the pastor and her counsellor was more for her own emotional well-being than her spiritual well-being. The court found no threat to her right to religious freedom by having the counsellor testify. As well, the court found that Adele had made the confession voluntarily without prior consideration to confidentiality. The court dismissed her appeal.

She tried the Supreme Court of Canada next. In their decision regarding the protection of a religious communication, the justices stated:

> "A first step involves verifying whether the communications fall into the pastor-penitent category at all. The communications must be intended to be of a religious or spiritual nature. This involves inquiring into: (1) whether the communication involves some aspect of religious belief, worship or practice; (2) whether the religious aspect is the dominant feature or purpose of the communication; (3) whether the communication would have been called into being without the religious aspect; and (4) whether the religious aspect of the communication was a good faith manifestation of a religious belief, worship or practice, or whether it was colourable."

They decided that Adele's confession did not meet the test for a privileged communication because it was not inherently private and did not stem from a religious practice or was part of a religious act. Again her appeal was denied. Regardless, Adele's case became the benchmark for applications in Canada in cases of confidentiality, especially those concerning religious freedom.

Adele Gruenke spent more than a decade behind bars. While incarcerated, she married another convict, Jeffery Breese, who, in 1982, held a woman and her two children hostage and shot an RCMP officer to death. Gruenke and Breese are both currently out on parole. At the time of printing, Jeff and Adele Breese were living in Winnipeg, and Adele was working as the office manager at the Manitoba branch of the Elizabeth Fry Society.

~

Chapter Ten

Yvonne Johnson

*"I have never denied that I was involved. I was angry at the possi-
bility that this man could be a child molester, sitting in my home.
I was angry because I couldn't talk to him about it. I was angry at
myself that I had to try to convince myself to get angry or mad
enough to even start to talk about it… And I couldn't walk away,
I couldn't run away. It was my home. It was my children. I just
didn't know what else to do…"*

–Excerpt of a 1996 taped statement by Yvonne Johnson ∽

A Bad Beginning

Everyday, the kids taunted her as she walked home from
school. "Indians on the warpath! Redskins coming!"
They plugged their noses. "Johnson germs! You'll get
contaminated from Johnson germs!" They would laugh and run
away from her brother Leon—tall and skinny but a great fighter.

It was the early '60s in Montana, and Natives were not even allowed to drink in the bars.

Yvonne Johnson is, in fact, only half Native. Her mother, Cecilia, was a great-great-granddaughter of the famous Plains Cree chief, Big Bear. Big Bear quickly established himself as "troublesome" for the British, who approached the great chief with Treaty 6, a treaty that laid out a land settlement that would entitle the Natives in the area to a piece of land one-third larger than the entire United Kingdom. Big Bear refused to sign the treaty at first, but when starvation forced his people back to "their" land when the buffalo became scarce, he was forced to sign in exchange for food from the North West Mounted Police. Over half a century later, his great-great-granddaughter would be kicked off the reservation at Red Pheasant, Saskatchewan, for marrying a white man.

Clarence Johnson was a big man from Great Falls, Montana. He met Cecilia when he left the United States Marines, having fought the Japanese at the end of the World War II. She had just left residential school, where the Catholic nuns had practised their own version of child rearing, which often involved child abuse. Johnson believes that Cecilia and Clarence were two broken people from the beginning of their relationship. Cecilia was only 16 when she met Clarence, and by the age of 17, she was pregnant. After being forced off the Red Pheasant Reserve, they moved to Butte, Montana, where Clarence worked in various mining jobs. The couple had a baby boy, Earl, followed four years later by another, Leon. Each October from 1958 to 1961, a girl was born—Karen, Minnie, Kathy and, finally, Yvonne. Five years later, Perry, the last of seven children, was born. Clarence drank a lot and often beat Cecilia. She fought back hard with vicious words.

"Both were so shoved into drunken violence all their lives that gradually, after years of living together, each new fight became little more than an extension of the last," Yvonne told Rudy Wiebe in his book chronicling her life, *Stolen Life*.

Yvonne was afflicted with the family curse. Her grandmother had a severe cleft palate, but Yvonne's was worse. As a baby, she had to be fed with an eyedropper, because the cleft separated her palate right through up to her nose. Her gums, the roof of her mouth, her top lip and her nose were split in two. Yvonne had to struggle to breathe and did not learn to talk until she was well past her toddler years and after numerous operations on the cleft. Her mother could never understand her and would often push her away to avoid having to try to figure out what the child was saying. Yvonne retreated into herself. "I learned very young to accept what I got. To hang my head, keep quiet and hide behind my hair. I learned fast about eye and body language, others' as well as my own. Look, don't talk. Move, don't speak."

Yvonne's family fell apart when Earl, the oldest brother, was found dead in a cell in the Butte jail. The Johnson family believes the town's crooked police killed Earl. Nothing ever came of their attempts to find the truth. However, the over-whelming corruption of the local police was announced in headlines in 1980, when regular civilians caught a well-known officer, Mickey Sullivan, as he was leaving a corner store that he had just robbed. Sullivan committed suicide, and two other officers were charged with numerous crimes, including burglary, arson, fraud, bombings and taking payoffs. All three officers were on duty the night Earl Johnson was found hanging from a plumbing pipe in the dungeon of the city jail.

Yvonne remembers, from an extremely early age, being subjected to horrific sexual abuse at the hands of her brother Leon, her father and her grandfather. The first attack took place when she was too young to speak. A friend of Earl's was babysitting when he found Leon "messing around" with Yvonne behind the fridge. He told eight-year-old Leon that he "wasn't doing it right." The teenager took Yvonne, put her on the table and took the clothes off the bottom half of her body. She started to cry, which caused her to choke, and she tried to get away, but the boy pulled her back and slapped her. He then started to penetrate her with his fingers, while explaining the process to Leon. Then he poked her in the anus. Yvonne kept reaching for her brother, but the babysitter just pushed her back onto the table. He forced Leon to hold Yvonne's feet while he abused her. Next, the babysitter took Yvonne into a bedroom and brought in Leon and three other young boys. He told the boys to "f*** her." He even pulled down their pants. The three boys jumped out the window. The babysitter started to beat Leon, yelling at him to attack his own sister. The man ended up sexually assaulting Leon until blood ran down Leon's legs. Then the babysitter put a diaper on Yvonne to soak up her blood. Earl later caught his "friend" trying to abuse another girl in the area and beat him up. But it was too late—the damage had already been done to Yvonne and Leon. From that time on, Leon felt he had a right to abuse Yvonne whenever he wanted. He continued to rape her right through adulthood.

Yvonne's mother Cecilia admits that Yvonne was abused. She once kicked her father-in-law out of the house when she caught him forcing Yvonne to "play" with him. But she does not accept that Leon abused Yvonne, not even after her daughter Karen charged him years later, and he served time in prison. Not even after Yvonne testified in court against her brother. However, from the time her daughters were five, she gave them warnings. "Don't hug your dad. Never hug your brothers, your male cousins or uncles or grandpas. If you do, you're asking for it. It's your own fault."

As she got older, Yvonne learned to drink. The drinking led to fighting, and she became well known in Butte as a good fighter. On other occasions, she would drink to the point of passing out—and then she usually ended up being raped. Yvonne remembers one time when a woman who befriended her in the bar took Yvonne to a house where five men had their way with her while she was passed out. The next weekend, the group bragged about it to her in the bar. Yvonne beat the woman senseless and never saw the group again. Yvonne ended up pregnant because of that terrible night, but she lost the baby after her mother set her up with a man, and the man's brother beat her severely. Her late teenage years were marred by drunkenness and suicide attempts. Yvonne shuttled back and forth between Butte, Winnipeg and the Red Pheasant Reserve in Saskatchewan, especially after her mother left her father.

One night, while out in Butte, Yvonne was "arrested" by the town police, then raped by four or five uniformed officers in a jail cell. Afterwards, when they locked her up, she yelled to the people passing by on the street, "Get my dad, Clarence Johnson!" Clarence came to the station and took his daughter home. He screamed at her for whoring around. Then he took off his belt, undid his pants and forced himself on her—and then begged her for forgiveness.

Yvonne was living in Winnipeg, a victim of her life and the mean streets, when she decided to get sober. She got a job and joined AA. She met a man with a job, and the pair moved to Uranium City, Saskatchewan—as far north as you can go without leaving the province. The man got a job as a blast hole driller. With all the money rolling in, the man started doing drugs and drinking all the time. He became abusive to Yvonne and watched every penny she spent. There was no way for her to get out. She ended up pregnant and had a daughter, Chantal, who also had the curse of the cleft palate.

The man lost his job, so Yvonne had to go to work. She was able to save some money and return to Winnipeg, where her mother was living. The man followed her and kidnapped Chantal to try to make Yvonne return to him. She tried to lay charges against him, but the police didn't take her seriously. The man gave Chantal back after he realized he couldn't feed or take care of her. After visiting her sisters in Alberta, Yvonne's mother decided that was the place to be. She and Yvonne moved to Wetaskiwin just before Christmas 1983.

Yvonne found that she could easily make a home in their small apartment, receiving welfare to pay for her rent and food for herself and Chantal. Yvonne spent her days playing with her daughter on the floor, dressing her up in clothes from the local Goodwill store and teaching her to use the potty and hold her fork. Things were good for the first time in her life.

In late January 1984, Yvonne met Dwayne Wenger. He was white and the first man she'd ever opened up to. She told him about living in Montana and shuttling back and forth to Manitoba and Saskatchewan, and about her family and siblings, though she left out the parts about the abuse she had suffered. It was the first time she felt comfortable and safe around a man. The pair began seeing a lot of each other. He was kind and patient with her; he loved Chantal. But he was also an alcoholic. Yvonne did not mind his drinking too much because he was a quiet and happy drunk. She could accept him, just as he had accepted her. When Leon was released from prison—he'd spent a lot of his teenage and adult life in prison for one thing or another—he showed up on her doorstep. Yvonne could never say no to a relative. In fact, she had a long string of relatives going in and out of her apartment all the time she lived there. Within days, he wanted to have sex with his sister. She told him no. He said, "Other sisters do it, why not you?" Yvonne was scared for her daughter. She asked Dwayne if she could move in until Leon left, and he agreed.

Dwayne had a small but well-kept house just outside downtown Wetaskiwin. He was a house painter and worked hard to pay his mortgage—a far cry from the usual leeches and deadbeats that Yvonne had known. She worked to keep the house clean, help Dwayne keep his business going and clean Dwayne up when he occasionally peed himself while passed out. The couple had three children, the first of which he asked Yvonne to abort. James was born in December 1985. Yvonne was pregnant when Dwayne went to prison for six months on a charge of drunk driving and possession. Susan came along a little more than a year after James in February 1987.

But things started to change. Dwayne stayed away a lot more with work, and then with drinking. There were affairs and fights. Yvonne paid the rent on her apartment for one month for Leon, but then refused to pay any more. He moved into their garage and started working with Dwayne. The men became drinking buddies. However, when Leon decided to start selling drugs, Dwayne told him he had to go.

Yvonne's cousin, Shirley Anne, often came and stayed as well. She liked to party and had an affection for men in general, Dwayne specifically. She would often make advances to him, but he always brushed them off. She would flatter Dwayne, all the while criticizing Yvonne. Nothing worked, and Yvonne knew that Shirley Anne would eventually leave, but would always come back again.

In the fall of 1988, Dwayne took a job in Yellowknife. He found himself a girlfriend and moved in with her, though he still talked to Yvonne on the phone. That year, the Johnson kids all got together and went to a reunion in Saskatchewan. There, Leon raped Yvonne again. A few months later, when Dwayne was back home but out for the night, cheating on Yvonne with another woman, Leon raped Yvonne right in her own home. It was her birthday. From that night on, Leon raped Yvonne every chance he got, whenever Dwayne wasn't around. Yvonne tried to talk to Dwayne about it, but he never wanted to listen.

Spiralling Out of Control

On Tuesday, September 12, Shirley Anne phoned. She was drunk and had no place else to go. It took her less than 10 minutes to reach Yvonne's doorstep. She told Yvonne that her daughters had kicked her out of their apartment in Saskatoon. Yvonne asked where her youngest daughter, a two-year-old, was. Shirley told her that she had left the girl with Darlene, Yvonne's half-sister, who lived in Thunder Bay. She claimed that Darlene wanted the child. "Oh, sure," Yvonne thought, "Your sister really wants to take care of that poor little girl."

Shirley Anne hung around until mid-afternoon, when she asked Yvonne for bus fare to Edmonton. Yvonne agreed to give her the fare and was just about to take her to the station, when a neighbour pulled up. With her was Chuck Skwarok, a large, heavyset man in his 30s. Shirley Anne was immediately all over Chuck. She was "batting her eyes, giggling, flaunting her 'cock-teaser' tone," Yvonne remembers.

Chuck did not say much in return. When the neighbour and Chuck left, Shirley Anne said, "Well, I guess we missed the bus." She shrugged and walked back into the living room.

Later, another friend, Ernie Jensen, came over. As usual, the group had a few beers. Shirley Anne made Ernie her next target. Dwayne and Yvonne decided to go to bed early and left Ernie and Shirley alone to sleep in the living room. Shirley Anne had finally scored. The next day, Shirley Anne began drinking early in the day and apparently forgot about going to Edmonton. She spent another day at the house.

September 14, 1989, was a hot day in Wetaskiwin. The kids were playing outside when Chuck Skwarok pulled up outside Yvonne's house in his small Hornet hatchback. He was really upset because his girlfriend, Yvonne's neighbour, had almost died from a grand mal seizure and was in the hospital. Yvonne invited Chuck in for a beer.

The TV was on in the living room, and they heard a news report about a man hanging around schools and kids disappearing for a few hours and then being returned. The man was apparently taking children out of schoolyards, fondling them while playing with himself, and then bringing them back. Yvonne, who lived right across from Parkdale School, thought of her kids and ran outside. No one was lingering in the bushes. She watched the children play for a minute, and then realized that her youngest, Susan, wasn't there. She ran to the garage where Ernie was fixing the freezer, but the girl wasn't there, either. Yvonne ran back into the house and saw Shirley Anne holding Susan. Susan was trying to get away from Shirley. Her little dress was pulled up and her panties were down around her ankles.

"Baby!" Yvonne yelled. Startled, Shirley grabbed the girl's panties and pulled them back up. Yvonne asked what was going on, and Shirley told her that Susan was showing them a birthmark high on her thigh. Yvonne told Susan never to pull down her pants in public, around anyone.

Just then, the phone rang. It was Yvonne's neighbour at the hospital. She wanted cigarettes. Yvonne agreed to take them to her, but only if Chuck could drive her. The two went to the hospital, leaving Shirley Anne with the children. After visiting the hospital, Chuck dropped Yvonne off at home and mentioned he might drop by later. When she came in, the house was quiet. Yvonne asked Shirley where the kids were. "I sent all them brats packing," she said, referring to the neighbourhood kids that had been over playing, "and yours are in the basement. I locked them in there to protect them."

"Protect them from what?" Yvonne asked.

"From your 'friend' Chuck. I thought he might sneak back here and kidnap one of them."

"What are you talking about? I barely know him!"

"You ought to know him better. He could have kicked you out anyway, easy. What could you do, big bugger like that?"

Yvonne bent in close to her cousin. "What do you know?" she demanded.

"He told me this when all the kids were running around, back and forth. He was looking at them kinda funny. He said they had nice buns, and then, just out of the blue, he told me, 'My wife charged me for molesting my little girl.' And he was looking at one of the kids kinda funny when he says this, and I says, 'Well, did you?' And he told me the whole thing."

At first, Yvonne panicked. Then she saw smug satisfaction in her cousin's face and felt overwhelmed by the whole situation. Why would Chuck tell a stranger about molesting his kids? Yvonne just walked out of the house.

Shirley Anne spent the rest of the day trying to convince Yvonne that she was telling the truth, egging her on to believe that Chuck might try something with Yvonne's kids. When Ernie came in from the garage, she told him, too. No one believed Shirley Anne. She told them to call Chuck, bring him over to the house, and she would ask him right in front of them. They waved her off.

The trio began drinking again. Shirley Anne would not let the matter rest, and she began to get to Yvonne. Yvonne agreed to phone Chuck to ask if he was still coming over. She didn't want him in the house with her kids, just in case. The first time she called, he was sleeping. Shirley Anne kept at it. Yvonne called again, and this time she spoke to Chuck. He wasn't going to come over because he was going fishing with his three cousins. Crisis averted.

Shirley Anne still wouldn't let it go, and she called Chuck. She flirted with him on the phone. She talked to him about his and his cousins' "tight buns," told him that Yvonne was heading to bed and convinced him to drop by. He agreed. Yvonne was worried. She knew that if Chuck came over with his three cousins and Shirley Anne confronted him, things could go very badly. In her mind, she was begging Dwayne to come home. She thought that everything would be okay if Dwayne was there. Yvonne, Shirley Anne and Ernie began drinking heavily.

Suddenly, Dwayne came home. "What's going on?" he asked.

"Shit, ask Shirley Anne," Yvonne told him.

"Chuck is a kid diddler," Ernie told him.

Chuck showed up at the door a few minutes later, without his cousins, and Shirley Anne let him in. Shirley Anne, Ernie and Dwayne all sat down on the couch. Yvonne sat in the sofa chair to the right of Dwayne. Chuck took his beer to the kitchen and brought back a stacking kitchen chair. He sat down next to Yvonne, his back to the closed bedroom door where her kids were sleeping.

Ernie looked at Chuck and asked, "Do you like men or little boys?" Shirley Anne started barking questions at Chuck, not waiting for him to respond. Chuck leaned back in his chair, puzzled but not concerned—not until Dwayne leaned forward and told him to stop staring at his "balls." Suddenly there was yelling, mostly between Chuck and Dwayne. Shirley leaned over Yvonne and told her to ask Chuck about being a child molester, trying to prove she was right. Yvonne jumped up. Everyone stopped talking. Shirley Anne yelled out, "Tell them what you told me! Your wife hauled you into court. You were molesting your own girl! Tell 'em, you f***ing kiddy f***er!"

Chuck sat straight up in his chair, coming almost face to face with Yvonne. Feeling crowded, she panicked and pushed him away. He flew backwards, into the door of her children's room, which flew open. Yvonne grabbed the door and started slamming it on Chuck, who was lying halfway into the kids' room. He jumped up and pushed Yvonne back. She flew onto the coffee table and fell, smashing to the floor.

Yelling erupted around the room. Shirley Anne and Ernie shouted at Chuck, and he yelled back, defending himself, denying the accusations. Chuck tried to leave, but Shirley Anne grabbed him by the hair and yanked hard to make him stop. He tried to shake her loose and headed towards the door with Shirley holding on tight. Yvonne got up and tried to get between the two, tried to make Shirley Anne stop so that Chuck could leave. Chuck started fighting her as well. Yvonne yelled at them to stop, but Dwayne suddenly jumped in. "Let go of my wife," he hollered. Ernie joined the mêlée. All five were punching and kicking, right up against the door to the basement stairs. The door gave way, and Chuck toppled down the stairs.

The men followed Chuck into the basement. Shirley Anne shadowboxed around the kitchen along to the sounds of fighting from the basement. Suddenly there was silence. Yvonne looked down the stairwell. Out of the darkness came Chuck. He grabbed Yvonne by the ankle, but she shook him free. She started to hit him with the door to the stairs and gave him a huge welt in the middle of his forehead. In her mind, she was all that was standing between a possible child molester and her children. He grabbed her ankle again and jerked her down into the stairwell. She grabbed onto a box hanging on the wall, the only thing keeping her from falling down the stairs. Chuck still held her ankle. Then Ernie and Dwayne raced up the stairs and grabbed Chuck, all three men pulling down on Yvonne. She could no longer hold on, so she let go. The group tumbled to the bottom of the stairs and were joined by Shirley Anne. It was now four on one.

Yvonne says that the other three pounced on Chuck, while she stood in shock for a moment. "Ernie would, like, bull-dog him and run him up against the wall, and then Shirley Anne...would come up there and punch him right where his head was cut. She just made it bleed, punching him there."

There was punching, wrestling and blood—a lot of blood—everywhere. Yvonne jumped in and tried to stop the fight. She told Chuck she was going to clean him up and sent Shirley Anne to get some water. Shirley Anne brought back just a small amount, so Yvonne went and got more. She tried to clean up the blood, but it kept coming. Then she looked Chuck in the eye. "And there was something about his eyes...something happened inside me.... And I could smell his sweat mixed with the water. I don't know, just the smell and his eyes." She stood back, called him a pig and poured the water on his head.

Ernie and Shirley Anne jumped on Chuck again, calling him an abuser. Yvonne broke them up again. She looked at Chuck and said, "Do you really know how it feels, to be raped as a child? Do you?" He didn't answer her. She screamed and ran away. Ernie yelled at Shirley Anne to take down Chuck's pants and started to undo his own. "I'll show him how it feels," he yelled. Yvonne told him not to "filthy" himself. Shirley Anne handed Ernie a steel table leg. Yvonne says that she knew that they were going to assault Chuck, so she took the table leg while either Dwayne or Ernie held Chuck in a headlock, and pretended to rape Chuck with it. She thinks they all believed that she had. She then said, "There. Let him go. Let him go now."

But then one of the group asked him if he was the guy from the news, the one molesting the kids from the schools. Chuck started crying. Ernie started beating Chuck again. By then Chuck had no clothes on the lower half of his body. Yvonne says she snapped and couldn't stand his nakedness. She went upstairs and got a knife from the kitchen. She used it to cut off a piece of telephone wire. She had intended to use it to tie Chuck up but was too drunk to stand still enough to tie Chuck's hands behind his back. Filled with a sudden rage, she called Chuck a child molester and wrapped the cord around his neck. It came undone within seconds. Ernie pushed Chuck up against a pipe in the basement. Chuck sat down and put his hands around the pipe. Ernie tried to tie him up, but the cord he had was too thick. Again the group asked Chuck if he was a child molester. He started to cry. He told them he would stop drinking and get help.

All hell broke loose. Yvonne shouted for Dwayne, an ex-boxer, to knock Chuck out. He tried, but Chuck was too strong. Ernie said, "I'll knock him out." He came over and kicked Chuck in the back of the head. Yvonne heard a loud crack. Then Shirley Anne did the same. Chuck emitted a gurgling sound.

Ernie wrapped a cord around Chuck's neck and dragged him around the basement. When he stopped, Dwayne stood on

Chuck while Shirley Anne wrapped the cord around Chuck's neck again and pulled. Ernie got another chair leg and sodomized Chuck. Dwayne noticed that Chuck had peed on the floor. To no one and everyone Dwayne stated, "He's dead."

The Aftermath

The group carried Chuck's body out of the basement and dumped it unceremoniously in the back of his own car. Yvonne left the house, apparently elected to get beer. She took her van and went to the Wayside Inn buy off sales. She bought four cases of beer and, on the way out, called her father from a payphone. "Dad, I'm in bad trouble. Can you get hold of Mom to come get the kids? Something really bad…"

A man from the bar stepped out of the shadows and asked her if she was all right. Then two police officers began talking to her. She started to panic, wondering if the police had already been to her house. She backed away to get into the van, and the man from the bar climbed into the passenger seat. One of the officers leaned in and handed her the case of beer she had left on the pavement. He noticed blood on her crotch. "Hey, something wrong? Your old man beat you up? Who were you calling there? Look, there's blood on your pants. You get raped?"

Yvonne did her best to get away from the officers, even though it meant leaving with a stranger sitting in the passenger seat. Once they were away from the bar, she told him to get out. He refused. She kept driving, trying to figure out a plan. The guy in the passenger seat kept talking and talking. She decided to go home and let the men deal with him, but when she pulled up to the house, Chuck's Hornet hatchback was gone. "We put him in the back of his car!" The words were out before she thought them, "And now the car is gone!"

Her passenger had no idea what she was talking about, but when she tried to get out of the van, he stomped on her foot and drove off. When he stopped the van a block later, he dragged her out of the driver's seat. Now he was in control.

Lyle Schmidt started drinking Yvonne's beer as he drove aimlessly around the rural part of Wetaskiwin County. Finally he pulled over to let her pee. Before she could stand back up, he attacked her and sent her sprawling on the ground. She fought, but he knew she was too drunk to put up much of a fight. He raped her in the back of the van. Lyle told police that Yvonne told him all about the killing while he drove around with her that night. He said that he drove her home, and when they arrived, Ernie was asleep on the couch. When Dwayne came out, he told Yvonne and Lyle, "It's done with. We got rid of him." And then he went back to bed.

Lyle claimed that Yvonne led him to the basement and showed him the blood and the knife, which he turned over to police. Yvonne has limited memories of what happened after Lyle raped her.

At 7:30 the next morning, a packer at the city dump found Chuck Skwarok's half-naked body in a pile of garbage. Half an hour earlier, Lyle had signed a two-page statement informing police that there might have been a murder in town.

Police arrested Dwayne at 11:38 AM, outside Parkdale School where Chantal was in class. Seven minutes later, police broke down the door of Yvonne's house and arrested her. Although Yvonne told the police she had been raped by Lyle Schmidt, the hospital only took her blood. They never performed an examination or checked for signs of rape.

Yvonne exercised her right to remain silent. Dwayne, and later Shirley, did not. Dwayne told the whole story to the police shortly after arriving at the station. From his statement, warrants went out for the arrest of Ernie and Shirley Anne. Shirley, after being arraigned along with the other three on first-degree murder charges, quickly made a deal with the Crown to testify against Ernie and Yvonne. The judge decided to try Dwayne first, then Shirley Anne, followed by Yvonne and Ernie together.

Dwayne pleaded guilty to second-degree murder. Judge Nina Foster sentenced him to life in prison, but with the possibility of parole after 10 years. A week later, Shirley Anne stood in front of a judge and pleaded guilty to aggravated assault. Perhaps because she was going to testify against Yvonne and Ernie, or maybe because her lawyer was just very good, the judge and the Crown, surprisingly, accepted the plea. She only received a one-year sentence with five years probation.

Ernie and Yvonne went to trial together on March 4, 1991, and pleaded not guilty to the first-degree murder charge. Although the two wanted to plead guilty to a lesser charge, the Crown prosecutor would not agree to accept the plea. Yvonne's lawyer asked that she be tried separately from Ernie. The judge refused. Her lawyer also attempted to have the trial moved to a place where racial tension and the media circus were not as prevalent. Again, the judge turned him down.

Shirley Anne presented her version of events at the trial. She told the court that Yvonne had talked about killing Chuck as soon as she called him that night. She told the court that it was Yvonne who had wanted Chuck to come over and had been the ringleader in his beating. Lyle Schmidt testified that Yvonne had told him that she had killed Chuck because she caught him molesting her daughter. He told the court that she had beat Chuck up and shoved a knife up his rectum. He stated that while they were driving around, Yvonne had asked him for help disposing of the body. He also said that having sex was Yvonne's idea, that they had discussed it, and that she had taken off her own clothes.

Although the forensic evidence showed that Chuck had died from a blow to the head and did not have any damage to his rectum, certainly not the kind a knife would do, the jury must have believed both Shirley Anne and Lyle's testimony.

The jury took only one day to reach its verdict. Yvonne Johnson was found guilty of first-degree murder—the first Native woman in Canada ever to be convicted of that crime. Ernie Jensen was found guilty of second-degree murder and sentenced to 10 years. Yvonne got life with no chance of parole. She appealed her sentence, but the appeal was rejected. However, in 2005, Yvonne succeeded in her bid for early parole at a faint hope hearing. The court decided that Yvonne would be eligible for parole on October 5, 2005.

After writing to author Rudy Wiebe in 1992, Yvonne shared her story in the book, *Stolen Life: Journey of a Cree Woman*. The book became a bestseller, and Rudy Wiebe won the Saskatchewan Book Award for Non-Fiction and the VIACOM Canada Writer's Trust Non-Fiction Prize. Finally, in January 2008, Yvonne was granted parole on the condition that she abstain from alcohol and attend psychological counselling.

~

Chapter Eleven

Jamie Gladue and Deanna Emard

Reuben Beaver was a cad. His fiancée, Jamie Gladue, was five months pregnant, but he was sleeping with her sister. During his fiancée's 19th birthday party, he slipped out for some action. He didn't count on her finding out—or killing him.

Wilfred Shorsen was ashamed of the bruises. He hid the marks on his neck. Covered them with turtleneck sweaters. He was vague to family about the other marks on his body. A small but proud man, he loved his daughter and tried to work through the problems with his wife. Family members tried to help him, but he would never admit the hell he was going through at home. It all came to a deadly end when he was stabbed through his broken heart by his wife, Deanna Emard.

Both of these women responsible for killing their partners were aboriginal. Their cases helped define a new clause in the Canadian Criminal Code, Section 718.2(e). ❧

JAMIE'S STORY

J amie Gladue was born in McLennan, Alberta, in 1976. Women in the area often bonded closely with each other while their men were out working on the oil rigs or putting in long hours in the fields. The town in northern Alberta was near a Cree reserve and was home to many band members who lived off the reserve. Originally a French settlement, the town was also home to many Métis Albertans. Jamie's mother, Marie Gladue, was Cree, and her father, Lloyd Chalifoux, was Métis—a typical union for the area.

Jamie had eight siblings. Their house was crowded, and the family was poor. When Jamie was 11, her mother left, leaving her father to raise Jamie and her siblings. Jamie's mother died in 1990 in a car accident. Three years later, when Jamie was 17, she moved in with Reuben Beaver, a Cree from Wabasca, Alberta, who was a year older than she was. In June 1994, Reuben was convicted of assaulting Jamie and given a 15-day intermittent sentence and a year's probation. She was pregnant at the time of the assault, and soon she was the unwed mother of a new baby girl, Tanita, born in early 1995. In August of the same year, Reuben, Jamie and Tanita all moved to a townhouse on Highland Boulevard in Nanaimo, British Columbia. Jamie's father and two of her sisters, Tara and Bianca, had moved to Nanaimo earlier and were living in the same complex. Bianca, Jamie's younger sister, was living with Reuben's younger brother.

Reuben and Jamie got engaged, and by September 1995, Jamie was pregnant again.

Jamie Gladue turned 19 on September 16, 1995. She was five months pregnant, but that didn't stop her from celebrating with a few beers. Her friends and family had come for her party. They all gathered at the apartment of Georgette Atleo, a friend that Jamie and her family had met through the Tillicum Haus Native Friendship Centre in Nanaimo. As the night wore on, Jamie mentioned to Georgette and her sisters that she thought Reuben was sleeping with her sister Tara. "He's only the second guy I've ever slept with, but he fooled around in Alberta lots." Her friends didn't want to get involved, but she became more and more persistent. She said, "The next time he fools around on me, I'll kill him."

The Atleo sisters began sharing their stories of the guys who had cheated on them. They urged her to leave him, "You don't need someone who's gonna fool around on you." Jamie got angrier with Reuben and decided she wanted to catch him cheating. She leaned over to Georgette and said, "Hey, you hit on Reuben and see if he'll go with you."

"Don't be crazy."

"No, really. Then I'll know for sure. I'm gonna kill him."

"No way. Leave me out of it." Her friend absolutely refused to be part of Gladue's set-up.

Jamie sulked for a bit. Soon, Tara left the party to go to her place to get something. Shortly afterwards, Reuben followed Tara. When he did not come back, Jamie became irate with her sister and her fiancée. "He's going to get it. He's really going to get it this time," she said to her friends. She asked Georgette to come with her to find Reuben and Tara. They ran out of the party and looked all over the townhouse complex for the pair. First, they went to Jamie's. It was locked, and she did not have a key with her. Tara's townhouse was also locked. Jamie got very upset. She and Georgette went back to the party, but they didn't let the issue rest. The two women left the party several times but couldn't find Tara and Reuben. Jamie, positive they were together, went to look for them one last time.

This time, she found Tara's door unlocked. She knocked, but no one answered, so she let herself in. Tara and Reuben were coming down the stairs inside the townhouse. Jamie, knowing she was right about Reuben's cheating, was furious with her sister. "How come you didn't let me in?" Tara just looked away. "Just wait till Dad finds out!" Jamie confronted her sister. "How could you? How could you do this to me?" Tara, shocked at being found out, did not respond, but simply ran out the back door of the townhouse.

Reuben and Jamie left Tara's townhouse and went back to their own. They started arguing loudly—loud enough to wake their neighbour, Anthony Gretchin.

"I know you are cheating on me, you bastard! How could you do this to me? With my sister!" she screamed at him. "I am sick and tired of you fooling around with other women."

Reuben, drunk and completely unapologetic, responded, "You are fat and ugly. You're not as good as the others." He sneered at her.

Anthony, the next-door neighbour, heard the sounds of physical fighting, banging, smashing and a lot of shouting. "It sounded like someone got hit and furniture was sliding, like someone being pushed around." He went on to say, "The fight lasted five to 10 minutes. It was like a wrestling match." He went to his door to confront the pair and tell them to calm down and be quiet. Instead, he heard the door to their town-house slam. Anthony opened his door and saw Jamie run past. Reuben was banging on Tara's door shouting, "Let me in! Let me in!"

Jamie got closer to Reuben. "You'd better run," she said, brandishing a large butcher knife at him. Reuben didn't move. Anthony watched in horror as Reuben suddenly screamed out in pain and dropped to the floor. Blood poured out of a hole in his chest and pooled on the ground around him. Jamie started bouncing up and down, pointing at Reuben and taunting, "I got you! I got you!" Anthony would later say that she was acting like a child playing tag. Then she turned and walked back to her townhouse. As she passed, Anthony heard her say, almost to herself, "I got you, you f***ing bastard." It was 1:50 AM on September 17, 1995.

During a preliminary hearing, the court heard evidence that Jamie had stabbed Reuben before they went into the hallway, apparently during the scuffle in the apartment. Police collected a paring knife from the living room floor. Tests on the knife found Reuben's blood. His upper arm had small cuts, apparently made by the paring knife. The defence entered evidence of bruising on Jamie's arm and around her neck and collarbone, hoping to have the court rule that she was a battered woman. The trial judge disagreed and said that the facts did not show that she was a "battered or fearful wife."

At the time of the killing, Jamie had a blood alcohol level of between .155 and .165, twice the legal driving limit.

The judge in the preliminary hearing ordered a trial, which began in February 1997, 17 months after the murder. Pending trial, Jamie was released on bail and went to live with her father. She gave birth to her second child on January 25, 1996, and named him Reuben Ambrose Beaver in honour of his father. She began alcohol and drug counselling at the Tillicum Haus Native Friendship Centre and completed grades nine and ten. As well, she was diagnosed with a hyperthyroid condition. She had to undergo radiation to kill some of her thyroid gland and took supplements to control her condition, which is known to cause exaggerated reactions to emotional situations. During the time she was out on bail, she also pleaded guilty to breaching the condition of abstaining from consuming alcohol. Apparently, her counselling was not working.

When she went to trial for second-degree murder in February 1997, she was again several months pregnant. Shortly after the jury was chosen, Jamie decided to enter a plea of guilty of manslaughter.

During the sentencing hearing, Jamie's counsel asked for a suspended sentence as she was not a danger to the public and deterrence was not needed. The Crown argued that the circumstances of the case made it fall into the middle range for sentencing, and the sentence should be three to six years. When the judge asked Gladue if she had anything to say, she apologized for the murder, stating that she had not meant to kill Reuben and apologizing to his family.

During his sentencing remarks on February 13, 1997, the judge summarized what he considered to be the mitigating factors in the case: Gladue's age, her supportive family, her alcohol and drug counselling and academic upgrading, her hyperthyroid condition, and her remorse and distress about the killing. He then went on to say:

> "Against these mitigating factors are some aggravating factors. They are these:
>
> 1. She stabbed the deceased twice, once in the apartment with a paring knife, and then she chased after the deceased with a large knife and stabbed him again.

2. She had committed an offence of particular gravity to take another person's life, carrying with it a maximum sentence of life imprisonment. This conduct is irrevocable, and in this case, the deceased was pursued out of his apartment, along a walkway of some 60 feet [18 metres] to the door of another apartment as he tried to escape the accused.

3. As she pursued the deceased, she warned him to run away. She was intent on harming him seriously, and in fact did so. After the event, she said, "I got you, you f***in bastard," which indicates she intended to do so, though she lost her self-control.

4. The accused was not afraid of the deceased that night; rather, he was afraid of her."

The judge asked Jamie about McLennan, the town where she was raised. Specifically, he asked her if she was an aboriginal person and whether or not McLennan was an aboriginal community. She replied that she was Cree, but that McLennan was "just a regular community." No arguments were put forth for consideration of her aboriginal heritage.

Finally, the judge concluded:

"This is a very serious offence. The accused has taken the life of another person. She was provoked by his conduct and his statements, but she lost her self-control and stabbed the deceased twice in two different locations. She found a larger knife and pursued the deceased with it after he had left the apartment, and she killed him with it. For that conduct, despite the mitigating factors and the provocation, I conclude the appropriate sentence is three years. In serving that sentence, the accused will have a better opportunity to rehabilitate herself through alcohol treatment. If she is in custody, she will be deprived of alcohol, which will be better for herself and her unborn child. She will be able to take advantage of the good facilities available to upgrade her education while in custody."

In addition to the three-year sentence, the judge also gave her a 10-year prohibition on owning or using a firearm.

Jamie quickly appealed her sentence—because she was Native.

DEANNA'S STORY

Deanna Margaret Emard was born into a Métis family in 1970 in the Vancouver area. Her childhood was not happy. Emard's father, struggling with having to support a wife and four kids, left when she was very young. Her mother tried to keep the family on track, but tragedy struck again and again. Drug and alcohol addiction ran rampant through her family, resulting in her uncle's death during a drinking binge and her sister dying of a drug overdose. One of her two brothers got into a fight late one night and was badly beaten. He suffered brain injuries so terrible that he was severely debilitated for the rest of his life.

Deanna tried to get away from the stigma of her early life. When she was 20, she met Wilfred Shorsen. They were an odd-looking couple. Wilfred was an average height of 175 centimetres, but very thin at only 65 kilograms. Deanna, on the other hand, was much larger than her spouse at 183 centimetres and 115 kilograms. But the pair quickly became enamoured of one other and were often overtly affectionate, despite a 12-year age gap. They got married and eventually had a beautiful little daughter, Natasha, in 1993.

Shorsen was a Haida from the Queen Charlotte Islands in northern British Columbia. Famous for their art, especially carvings, the Haida are well known even though they live in a secluded location. Many band members have started to drift away into the larger centres of the province, as was the case for Shorsen's family. Most of his relatives moved to the Vancouver area, which was where Wilfred met Deanna. One of 12 children, Wilfred had a large, close-knit family. At first, they accepted Wilfred's new, young wife, but then they began to notice the bruises. His sisters asked him about his injuries, but he always dismissed them as accidental. His family became suspicious.

On January 25, 1997, Wilfred, Deanna, and their daughter, Natasha, went to a birthday party for Shorsen's niece. Many of his relatives were there and, as usual, beer flowed freely. Wilfred and Deanna were both drinking. Sometime after midnight, the birthday party wound down, and Wilfred, Deanna and Natasha went to his brother Herbert's home. The little girl went to sleep on the living room couch, while the adults kept drinking and talking well into the early hours of the morning of January 26. At some point they all fell asleep, though no one can remember when. Herbert remembers his brother being "pretty intoxicated" that night and well into the early morning. Deanna was drunk as well.

Some time after passing out, Wilfred woke up and decided that his family needed to go home. He woke his sleeping wife. They picked Natasha up off the couch and carried her to the car while she slept. Wilfred started the car and pulled away from the house. Only a short distance later, Deanna decided that he was too drunk to drive and forced him to pull over so that she could take over the driving. Wilfred, knowing that she was also drunk, but possibly afraid of her, decided to let her drive, though he did not let the matter rest. The two argued the rest of the way home.

When they arrived at their East Vancouver home, Deanna took Natasha out of the car and put her to bed. Wilfred stayed in the vehicle. Deanna came back and the pair started arguing again. She claims that they were yelling at each other, and eventually, Wilfred got out of the car. However, instead of going into the house, the couple started fighting physically. Deanna started punching her much smaller husband. She hit him in the lip and, according to her, he "freaked out."

Deanna, ever dominant, decided the fight was over. She went inside and into the bedroom where her daughter was sleeping. She closed the bedroom door and went to bed. Wilfred started punching the wall outside the room. Suddenly the door flew open. Shorsen had kicked it in. "Me and baby were in the bedroom, and I just freaked out," Deanna remembers. She "flipped out" and chased Wilfred out of the bedroom. "You want to fight?" she screamed at him.

She ran into the kitchen and pulled a large butcher knife out of the drawer. Rushing at Wilfred, Deanna started physically fighting with him again. They wrestled in the kitchen and made their way into the dining area. Limbs and fists flew. Wilfred, despite his size, put up a good fight against his abusive wife. But then Deanna raised the knife above her head and, *Psycho* style, plunged the knife into her husband's chest. The blade entered just above his heart and severed a major artery. Deanna tried to stop the bleeding and called 911, but Wilfred quickly bled to death.

Deanna was immediately remorseful. In videotaped statements, she is in obvious distress over her husband's death. The couple had been together for a rocky eight years. Deanna stated that she did not mean to stab Wilfred. "We were both wrestling, and he was standing in front of me, and then it just went in right there, and he fell instantly."

However, in videotaped interviews with the police, Deanna used the above-the-head stabbing motion. The forensic pathologist, Dr. James Ferris, also supported this. He noted that the wound showed a downward angle of the blade, indicating a stabbing motion from above and into the chest. At one point in her interview, the police asked Deanna how many times she stabbed Wilfred, and she responded, "I didn't stab him. He fell. We were fighting. I don't even know if I would call it a stabbing. We were fighting, but it went in once, and that's it." Yet, Deanna continued to talk about the "stabbing" throughout the interview.

The case went to court in December 1998. The jury had to decide wheather Deanna was guilty of manslaughter or second-degree murder. They chose manslaughter. The case really started making headlines when Deanna's lawyer petitioned the court for leniency—because she was Native.

A SHORT HISTORY OF THE CANADIAN CRIMINAL CODE

In 1985, the Criminal Code was amended to include the following:

718.2 A court that imposes a sentence shall also take into consideration the following principles...

(e) all available sanctions other than imprisonment that are reasonable in the circumstances should be considered for all offenders, *with particular attention to the circumstances of aboriginal offenders.* (emphasis added by author)

Canada uses prison as a punishment more than almost any other developed nation. The government decided to try to change that. The first step was to add section 718.2 to the Criminal Code, and the second was to introduce a new bill to Parliament. Bill C-41 tried to address the need to look at alternatives to prison. In 1995, Minister of Justice Alan Rock brought the bill into the spotlight during a parliamentary debate. He stated that prisons need to be used for serious crimes, but for other types of offences, different options should be tried. In his arguments, he stated, "When appropriate, alternatives must be contemplated, especially in the case of Native offenders." Later, in the House of Commons, he stated:

> "The reason we referred specifically there to aboriginal persons is that they are sadly over-represented in the prison populations of Canada…. Nationally, aboriginal persons represent about two percent of Canada's population, but they represent 10.6 percent of persons in prison. Obviously, there's a problem here. What we are trying to do, particularly having regard to the initiatives in the aboriginal communities to achieve community justice, is to

encourage courts to look at alternatives where it's consistent with the protection of the public—alternatives to jail—and not simply resort to that easy answer in every case."

The result of the passing of Bill C-41 was an addition to the Canadian Criminal Code in 1996, Part XXIII. This section outlines the purposes and principles of sentencing and the factors to be considered by a judge when sentencing an offender. Taken together, Part XXIII and Section 718.2(e) lay out a guideline that clearly instructs judges to view aboriginal offenders differently than other offenders because of the uniqueness of their culture and history.

The Supreme Court of Canada ruled on the interpretation of these sections in April 1999 as part of their ruling on an appeal by Jamie Gladue. In their ruling, the court clearly asserted the effect these sections have on sentencing. They argued that the purpose of Section 718.2(e) was to amend the "serious problem of overrepresentation of aboriginal people in prisons [in Canada]." They went on to say that sentencing judges needed to look at traditional options, such as healing circles and community interventions, to assist in the rehabilitation and sentencing of offenders. The court was clear in stating that each offender had to be looked at for each individual offence, because no two cases would ever be identical. But when looking at aboriginal offenders, the courts had to make every effort to use alternative sanctions when available. As well, whether an offender was living on or off reserve, in a large urban centre or a small community, all non-imprisonment options had to be evaluated. The justices also made note of how systemic factors such as racial profiling and access to legal assistance influence the number of aboriginal offenders before the courts. However, in response to public outcries of the "get out of jail free" provision, the justices stated, "Section 718.2(e) is not to be taken as a means of automatically reducing the prison sentence of aboriginal offenders; nor should it be assumed that an offender is receiving a more lenient sentence simply because incarceration is not imposed."

Both Jamie Gladue, guilty of manslaughter in the killing of her adulterous husband, and Deanna Emard, guilty of manslaughter for killing her abused husband, became benchmark cases. Almost every case of an aboriginal offender in the Canadian court system today, particularly in manslaughter and murder cases, refers back to the judgements made in the Gladue and Emard cases.

JAMIE GLADUE'S APPEAL

Jamie Gladue appealed her three-year prison sentence to the Court of Appeal for British Columbia, and the case was heard in late May 1997. Her counsel argued before three judges that the sentencing judge had overemphasized the need to denounce and deter Gladue and had not taken her Native status into account. As well, they argued that Reuben Beaver had been abusive, and her sentence did not reflect her situation.

The appeal argued that the sentencing court had erred when it decided that her status as an aboriginal offender was not relevant because Gladue was living off the reserve. One of the appeal court judges agreed that the trial judge should have considered her Native status as a factor in his decision. However, the two other judges argued that they felt the sentencing judge had considered Gladue's aboriginal status and deemed it to be a non-issue in the case. In light of the whole picture, the court dismissed the appeal in a split two-to-one decision, so Gladue appealed to the Supreme Court of Canada.

Leading up to the ruling by the Supreme Court, major newspapers across Canada screamed about the "get out of jail free" card. Headlines such as "My Race Is an Issue" in the *National Post* were common in the Opinion sections of many papers. Gladue's case was setting a precedent—one that was causing a huge commotion. Letters to the Editor sections became a springboard for angry Canadians who felt that justice was no longer blind to race, some even arguing that it was a disadvantage to be non-aboriginal. Others wrote in about the hardships that a lot of Native people experience in Canada and the unique challenges they face on a daily basis. Lawyers and laypersons all seemed to have opinions.

The Supreme Court Justices had the difficult task of combining the two sections of the Criminal Code, 718.2(e) and Part XXIII, and jointly interpreting their meaning. Although the sections had been applied during sentencing for other cases, this was the first case to make it all the way to the Supreme Court.

In their decision, the court clarified how to apply the sections to sentences, stating that an aboriginal person's history needed to be taken into account; appropriate, non-imprisonment, sentences should be used whenever possible; sanctions outside prisons could be more punitive than incarceration; and systemic factors had to be addressed. Sentencing judges now had a specific directive as to how to apply sentencing options and principles to aboriginal offenders.

For Jamie Gladue, the Supreme Court agreed that the sentencing judge had not given enough weight to her Native status. However, the justices felt that the case was a serious one because it involved a death. Because of the violent nature of the crime, the three-year sentence was deemed appropriate, regardless of Gladue's heritage. They dismissed Jamie's appeal, and she completed her three-year sentence in 2002.

DEANNA EMARD'S APPEAL

"Woman Cites Métis Heritage as Reason for Light Sentence," the *National Post* cried on January 6, 1999. Emard's lawyer, Peter Wilson, was not shy in speaking to the press about his upcoming case. "I'm going to ask the court to consider [her aboriginal offender status] as a mitigating circumstance." The Vancouver Métis Association also stood behind Deanna. "In the two years she's been before the courts, she's taken her drug and alcohol counselling, she's been active in our preschool and active in our community affairs," Paul Stevenson, the association president stated. "We will be asking the court…that she be released to us, to her community, where she has good family support."

In court, Wilfred Shorsen's family certainly did not give Deanna any leniency for her Métis status. Twelve victim impact statements were filed. The statements were filled with love for Shorsen, citing him as a valuable member of the large family. Some also expressed an outright hatred for Deanna as well as references to Wilfred being a battered husband.

The court also received numerous letters of support from, among others, Deanna's doctor, Natasha's social worker, the president of the Vancouver Métis Association, the coordinator of Natasha's preschool, Natasha's psychologist, Deanna's bail supervisor and the Job Start program manager. They all agreed that Emard was devoted to her child, she was extremely remorseful and she continued to be a good mother.

In his sentencing decision, Justice Williamson stated that the forensic pathologist had testified that the wound was consistent with a stabbing motion, and Emard re-enacted the same motion during her confession to police. Despite Emard's own admission to stabbing Shorsen, the pathologist was "not able to determine whether she actually stabbed him in a fit of anger or whether…they were wrestling and the knife just went in." He went on to state, "These were two people, one of whom, as it was put, was 'freaked out,' and the other one who was extremely angry, who were tussling and wrestling. In those circumstances, anything can happen."

Justice Williamson also cited Gladue's case in his duty to take into account Emard's aboriginal background. He said, "Emard had led in some respects, her good marriage not withstanding, a very unhappy life" and that her history was characteristic of many aboriginal people in Canada. Although he felt that the case "cried out for denunciation," he also felt it was not likely Emard would commit such a crime in the future and that she need not be removed from society as she was not a danger. On January 19, 1999, Justice Williamson sentenced Deanna Emard to two years less a day to be served in the community. She maintained custody of her then five-year-old daughter.

The next day, newspapers across Canada carried the decision. Wilfred's family was outraged. "She doesn't even go to jail!" Shorsen's sister Mabelle cried. Mabelle had seen her younger brother shortly after the attack. He was slumped backwards on his haunches in the basement suite that he and Deanna shared. Although he was covered in blood, she could see fresh bruises on his arm, face and thigh. His nose was swollen, and he had fading bruises on his body as well, silently testifying to the ongoing abuse he had suffered. "He didn't ask to die. He didn't bring this on himself. It's a slap on the wrist."

Mabelle, Haida herself, was angry at Deanna's reliance on being aboriginal. "Alcohol is not an excuse, and neither is being a Native," she said. "There should be justice for everyone, not one system for Indian and Métis people and one for white people."

On January 21, two days after the sentencing, Michelle Mandel wrote an article for the *Toronto Sun* slamming the decision. In "Get Out of Jail Free Card for Natives?" Mandel stated, "In Canada, there is not justice for all. If you are Native, you have a better chance of getting away with murder."

In the article, Wilfred's brother Herb disagrees outright with the sentence. He said that Emard never mentioned any Native heritage until it was time to be sentenced for killing his brother. "We all came from impoverished families, but we don't go around killing our partners. How can we teach our children any different when the message they're getting is it's okay for us to grab a knife and stab someone?"

Deanna Emard completed her conditional sentence in 2001 while residing with her mother, her daughter and the son of her deceased sister. Today she lives in the Lower Mainland of British Columbia.

~

Chapter Twelve

Karla Homolka

Their story is infamous, their crimes horrific—the handsome couple from Ontario who raped and killed schoolgirls for fun. One of Canada's most controversial women, Karla Homolka tops the list as the most infamous deadly Canadian woman. ∾

∾

Karla Homolka was always pretty and popular. Her blonde hair and creamy skin were made for fame. Yet it was her sinister nature and need to please that would make her famous. Born on May 4, 1970, to Karel and Dorothy Homolka, Karla was the first of three daughters. The family was not well off, but Karel made enough money as a travelling salesman so that Dorothy could stay home with her girls. The family lived in small apartments and a St. Catharines, Ontario, trailer park before moving in 1978 to a house with a large yard on 61 Dundonald Street in a subdivision of the town.

Karla did well in school, often averaging over 80 percent in her high school courses. Her IQ was measured at 131 in elementary school—140 gets a person into Mensa. However, in grade 12, Karla decided to start working full time at the Number One Pet Store and take only a handful of the courses she still needed to graduate. As part of her job, Karla was invited to a conference in Toronto. She took along her friend and co-worker, Debbie Purdie.

Debbie and Karla went out on the town for the evening and found a pair of guys to spend their evening with. Paul and Van were just about to call it a night when they met up with the young women. Karla invited the men to their hotel room and delivered as well as she had led him to believe. The first night she met Paul Bernardo, Karla knew she would marry him.

Paul Bernardo was almost six years older than Karla. His childhood had an undercurrent of sexual abuse. His father had abused Paul's sister for most of her young life. Finally, when her father started abusing her own daughter in the same way, nearly 30 years later, she laid charges of sexual abuse against him.

Paul did not find out until his late teens that the man he had always called "Dad" was actually not his father. Paul's mother, Marilyn, had conceived Paul during an affair. Marilyn, who had been given up for adoption at a young age, had also suffered sexual abuse as a child, perhaps explaining her ability to turn a blind eye to the suffering of her own daughter. One day, as Paul was starting grade 10, Marilyn threw a picture at Paul of a man who looked just like him. She suddenly declared that Ken Bernardo was not Paul's father, the man in the picture was.

From a young age, Paul had a tremendous amount of self-esteem. He was fastidious with his appearance and easily charmed many a woman into his bed. As he grew older, his girl-friends found him to be extremely possessive and rough, often abusive. One girlfriend remembers Paul being excited by the fact that she was a virgin and he would get to take that from her. However, after the first time, he was only interested in anal sex. It was a pattern that repeated for years to come.

Paul and Karla immediately began dating following their first encounter in Toronto. On their first date, Karla took him to the basement of her parent's home and produced a pair of handcuffs. Paul couldn't believe his luck when Karla said she wanted to be tied up and entered from behind. He asked her what she would think of him if he were to start raping women. Karla was all for it. So Paul, fulfilling a fantasy, began raping women on his drive to and from Karla's home.

Paul, who worked for a financial firm as a chartered accountant, would drive from Scarborough, where he lived, to St. Catharines at least a few times a week. He usually made the trip on Wednesdays and weekends, often staying overnight with Karla in her family's home—with her parent's approval, even urging. Dorothy and Karel found Karla's new boyfriend to be refined and charismatic. They approved of his treatment of their daughter—he took her out to fancy dinners and sent her large bouquets of flowers. He had a job with a prestigious firm and seemed to be a dream come true for the Homolkas, who had found Karla's recent foray into the world of teenage angst a trifle problematic. They didn't know that on his way home, he was stalking and raping women waiting at bus stops.

The "Scarborough Rapist" was attacking young women, usually schoolgirls. He talked throughout the rapes and asked his victims questions about their lives. He stole their identification, threatening to come find them if they talked to police, and made them shut their eyes while he ran away. Karla, during this time, often sent Paul love notes thanking him for being so perverted and declaring her undying love for him. One of the rape victims had a blurry memory of a woman being present during her rape, filming the whole thing with a video camera. Police thought she must have imagined it out of stress.

While police searched for the rapist, Paul and Karla fell more and more in love. Karla switched jobs to become a veterinary assistant at an animal clinic, but her new career was short-lived because the veterinarian at the clinic accused her of stealing ketamine, an anesthetic used on animals going into surgery. She wasn't out of work long and was soon hired by the Martindale Animal Clinic as a technician.

On December 9, 1989, Paul proposed to Karla. They planned their wedding for June 29, 1991. As the planning of an elaborate wedding began, Paul realized that his accountant's job would no longer support his lifestyle. He quit his job and began smuggling cigarettes and selling them on the black market.

On May 29, 1990, police released a photograph of the Scarborough Rapist to the media. People from Paul's old office, as well as a bank teller at Paul's bank, called police to report that the picture closely resembled Paul Bernardo. Lost among the other tips, Paul's name was added to a long list of look-alikes. Paul Bernardo dyed his hair the same day. It was months before police called Paul to give blood and saliva samples, and then they were filed away for 25 months before being sent for comparison. The officers did not think that the pleasant, polite young man could be involved in such heinous crimes. It was just another false lead.

That summer, Karla, knowing that Paul was upset with her for not being a virgin when they met, decided to give her 15-year-old sister, Tammy-Lynn, to Paul as a "present." First, she broke the blinds in her sister's bedroom so that Paul could watch her undress. Next, she pretended to be Tammy-Lynn as the couple had sex in the girl's bed. One night, Karla drugged Tammy with Valium. Paul and Karla snuck into Tammy's bedroom, where Paul masturbated beside Tammy's sleeping head, then tried to have sex with her. Tammy stirred, so Paul stopped, and Karla stepped in to give Paul oral sex beside the drugged teenager, while Paul pretended to be with Tammy.

Knowing that Paul was not happy with how the night with Tammy went, Karla had to go a step further. She started stealing halothane, a drug used on animals to put them to sleep during surgery, and another sleep aid, Halcyon, during her shifts at the Martindale Animal Clinic. As the drug dispenser for the clinic, it was easy.

In December 1990, Paul bought a new video camera. Plans for a night with Tammy-Lynn grew more specific. After several thwarted attempts, the opportunity presented itself on December 23. The family was all together. They had a few drinks, and the senior Homolkas went to bed, leaving Karla, Paul and Tammy watching a movie. The trio kept drinking, and Karla put Halcyon into Tammy's daiquiris. Soon, she was high from the sleeping pills mixed with alcohol and fell asleep on the couch. Paul set up his video camera as Karla poured halothane onto a cloth and held it over her sister's mouth and nose. Karla pulled down her sister's pants, and Paul immediately entered the young girl. Paul alternated between forcing himself on the girl and making Karla have oral sex with both him and Tammy. Karla alternated between violating the girl and pleasuring Paul. Suddenly, Tammy started to vomit. Paul tried to clear her airway, and then the two pulled Tammy into Karla's bedroom. Karla dressed her sister and realized that Tammy was not breathing. She called 911 while Paul performed CPR. It didn't matter—Tammy was dead.

Police were curious about the redness around Tammy's mouth and asked about drugs, but everyone in the family categorically denied that there were any drugs in the house. They were also a little surprised by Karla's need to immediately wash the blanket that Tammy had vomited on; the washing machine was running when the paramedics arrived at the house. But in the end, the police viewed Tammy's death as a tragedy in which a young girl had too much to drink at Christmastime and choked to death on her own vomit.

Paul went back to committing rape. Karla, the day after her sister's funeral, picked up more Halcyon. This time, with Karla's family gone from the house for the night, Paul brought a girl home and raped her in front of Karla. Later, he let the girl out of his car on the edge of town and went home to Karla. She pretended to be Tammy while they had sex in front of the video camera.

It wasn't until Karla and Paul moved into their own house that Paul started bringing girls home on a regular basis. Karla contacted a girl she used to work with at Number One Pet Centre. The girl, who looked remarkably similar to Tammy, was excited to spend time with the older, worldlier Karla. She was eager to start drinking when Paul and Karla offered her alcohol and, not being a drinker, did not know that the sour taste was unusual. Karla had laced the teenager's drinks with Halcyon, and, like Tammy, the girl fell asleep. Again, Paul and Karla made videos of their assaults on the girl. She would be a frequent, unknowing participant in the sex life of the couple.

On June 14, 1991, 14-year-old Leslie Mahaffy arrived home after her curfew to find that her parents had locked her out of the house. She stumbled upon Paul Bernardo while trying to find an unlocked entry point. Paul had seen Leslie attempting to get in the house and thought he could spy on her while she got ready for bed. They surprised each other as they rounded a back corner of the house and ran smack into each other. According to Stephen Williams in *Invisible Darkness: The Horrifying Case of Paul Bernardo and Karla Homolka*, Leslie was not scared of Paul at first. It wasn't until he pulled a knife on her after she asked him for a cigarette that she had any idea of the danger she was in. He held a knife to her throat and forced her to get in the car with him. He called Karla at home and woke her up, telling her that he had a surprise for her. She saw the girl as a reciprocal gift for the girl from the vet clinic. Karla went back to bed while Paul repeatedly raped the girl in their home. When Karla woke up and found her good champagne glasses had been used, she was angry. She decided to ignore the shut door to the spare bedroom and went on with her day.

Paul prepared Leslie for Karla. He made her take a shower, all the while filming her with the video camera. Leslie had been blindfolded all night and most of the day. When Karla got home, Paul presented Leslie to her. Karla and Paul spent the rest of the day raping Leslie Mahaffy together, capturing everything on videotape. Fifteen days later, a man and his wife out for a canoe ride came across blocks of cement. Inside the blocks were parts of the teenager. Although a lot of police resources were spent investigating the murder, there were no strong leads.

Around the same time that the police were pulling body parts out of the lake, the Bernardos were getting married. The elaborate ceremony and reception, attended by 150 guests, went off without a hitch.

On April 16, 1992, the day before Good Friday, Karla went looking for a new sex slave. Karla took the afternoon off work, and she and Paul waited for a victim outside a St. Catharines high school. When she spotted Kristen French walking home, Karla knew they had a good target. She called the girl over to the gold Nissan for directions. When Kristen came up to the car, Paul jumped out of the driver's seat and held a knife to the girl's throat. Kristen tried to fight, but Paul was too strong. He forced her into the car.

Again, Paul and Karla raped the young teenager. They originally kept her blindfolded and taped the episodes at length. At one point, Kristen vomited so hard that the blindfold fell off. Karla dutifully cleaned up the mess and then proceeded to feed her husband and their kidnapped rape victim dinner. Paul left Kristen and Karla alone while they talked about boyfriends, family and pets. Karla and Paul, implicitly understanding that the girl would never make it out alive, never bothered to blindfold Kristen again.

As the police searched for the missing teenager throughout the Easter long weekend, Karla and Paul played "sex games" with Kristen. Karla often filmed the assaults, giving verbal directions to Kristen. Kristen and Karla then put on a schoolgirl-style play for Paul, dressing in school uniforms, Kristen doing anything to keep her captors happy. While Paul was out for dinner, Kristen and Karla watched Kristen's father pleading for her safe return on the evening news.

A scrap-metal picker found 14-year-old Kristen's body in a ditch on April 30. She was nude, and her face had been beaten in and her hair shaved off to disguise her identity.

As 1992 drew to a close and 1993 was rung in, things in the Bernardo household were slowly falling apart. Although Paul was still bringing home women to have sex with and drugged yet another teenager unaware, he seemed to be having a mental breakdown and was often short-tempered with his wife. Paul began to openly make sexual advances to friends and family, often climbing into bed naked with overnight guests. He and Karla argued constantly, and the situation came to a head on January 4, 1993. Paul had just come back from a trip across the border and, for no apparent reason, beat Karla badly. Karla's mother got a call from two different anonymous people telling her she needed to go help her daughter. When Dorothy Homolka arrived at the vet clinic, she was shocked to see her daughter with two black eyes and various other injuries. Karla admitted that Paul had beaten her, but she insisted on continuing to work. Dorothy told Karla that she was going to take her home after work, but when she came back, Karla was gone. The Homolkas called Karla repeatedly, and finally, Paul answered the phone. Assuring Dorothy that everything was fine, he even put Karla on the phone. The next day, Dorothy went to the Bernardo's home to see her daughter. Karla was in even worse shape—Paul had beaten her again. Dorothy convinced Karla to leave Paul, so she packed some belongings. Then she told her mother that Paul had killed Tammy-Lynn. It confirmed a long-held suspicion of Dorothy's. Karla's mother took her to a friend's house and then to the hospital. At St. Catharines General Hospital, the emergency room doctor said it was the worse case of abuse he had ever seen. Police arrested Paul Bernardo for assaulting his wife.

Despite many reports of rapes associated with a gold Camaro (Paul drove a gold Nissan) and another woman giving the police a report about being stalked by a man in a gold car, even supplying his address and licence plate number, the police didn't connect Paul Bernardo to the rapes and deaths of teenage girls until February 1, 1993, when his DNA came back as a match to the Scarborough Rapist. Police immediately started surveillance on Paul. They also tried to talk to Karla but were rebuffed at every attempt.

Finally, one week later, Karla met with police. In a five-hour interview, she told them all about her abuse. Police officers took Karla's fingerprints and asked her about a Mickey Mouse watch she was wearing. She told them it belonged to her sister Lori, though she had actually stolen it from Kristen French. Police left with little information, but Karla immediately confessed to the aunt and uncle she was staying with that Paul was the Scarborough Rapist—and that he had killed

Kristen French and Lesley Mahaffy. Her relatives advised Karla
to contact a criminal lawyer.

Karla hired George Walker. She told Walker about the
sexual assaults, the videos and the killings. She wanted immunity.
Walker went straight to Ray Houlahan, the regional prosecutor,
and told him that Paul Bernardo was a killer and he wanted to
negotiate a deal for Paul's wife, who had been beaten and forced
to participate in the killings. Houlahan, not having the proper
authority to make such a deal, called Murray Segal, the Crown
prosecutor. Segal was not interested in granting immunity, but
thought that a deal could be reached.

On February 17, 1993, Paul Bernardo was arrested for
the killings of the two girls and for the Scarborough rapes.
Although police interrogated him for eight hours, he refused to
tell his side of the story. The next morning, Paul Bernardo
appeared in court and was remanded into custody. Police
searched Paul and Karla's home on February 19 and discovered
a list of all the Scarborough rapes, books of a sexually deviant or
extremely violent nature and a stack of videotapes. Mostly the
tapes were of television shows, but one contained video of
the Bernardos having sex with two unidentified women. The
tape clearly showed Karla involved and enjoying the acts, not
the beaten, abused wife she was portraying herself to be.

Regardless, on February 25, Karla agreed to a plea bar-
gain in which she would serve two 10-year prison sentences concurrently, hopefully in a psychiatric hospital, and be eligible for

parole in three years as long as she testified, truthfully, to the sexual assaults and murders. After a seven-week stay in a mental hospital where she underwent psychological testing, a new deal was reached. Although not formally included in the sentence, Karla got two more years for the rape and killing of her sister. It wasn't until the fall of 1994, when Paul Bernardo's original lawyer, Ken Murray, turned over the extensive video collection of the rapes of all the victims to the police, that the truth of Karla's involvement became known. Unfortunately the "deal with the devil" was done. There was nothing the prosecution could do. Karla testified against Paul in 1995 and was portrayed by the Crown as a helpless, abused wife, even though the Crown prosecutors knew that was not the case. Paul Bernardo received a sentence of life in prison and was later classified as a dangerous offender, making him ineligible for parole.

Karla, one of Canada's most controversial and infamous murderers, chose not to apply for parole any of the times she was eligible. Instead, she chose to complete her 12-year sentence. While in prison, Karla completed a degree in psychology through correspondence courses. Just prior to her release, Ontario's attorney general, Michael Bryant, pushed for a judge to place further restrictions on Karla, including staying away from previous victims, reporting her whereabouts to police, staying away from children under 16 and having no contact with Paul Bernardo. The restrictions interfered with Karla's new relationship with another inmate, Jean-Paul Gerbet, who had been convicted of killing his girlfriend in 1998. Karla and

Gerbet were seen kissing in the library of the prison. As well, Karla had a nude photo of the man in her cell. It wasn't the first relationship Karla had in prison—she also had a three-year lesbian relationship early in her sentence while incarcerated in the Joliette Institution. Lynda Veronneau, Karla's lover, released a book in 2006, *Lynda Veronneau: A l'ombre de Karla (Lynda Veronneau: In the Shadow of Karla)* detailing the pair's relationship. Karla's lawyer told reporters after the hearing that Karla was aware she could no longer communicate with Gerbet after being released, but that Gerbet would be deported as soon as he was released in 2008 anyway.

Upon being whisked out of the Ste-Anne-des-Plaines prison on July 4, 2005, at the end of her sentence—a day early to avoid the massive media spotlight—Karla went straight to the media. She sat down for a one-on-one interview on CBC. She said in French, which she spent years learning in prison, "I don't want to be hunted down. I don't want people to think I am someone who is dangerous, who will do something to their children." She expressed remorse for her crimes and asked to be left alone.

She moved to Montréal and appealed the restrictions placed on her. She won her appeal in November 2005 and was then free to talk to any of the victims or other inmates. Since then, she has tried to legally change her name to Emily Tremblay, one of the most common names in Québec, but has been turned down twice. She still has the right to try again.

In February 2007, Karla made front-page news once more after keeping fairly quiet in Montréal since her release. Newspapers in Québec reported that Karla had given birth to a baby. The press had also received anonymous letters stating that nurses had refused to care for her during the delivery of the baby. Although the hospital investigated the allegations, no evidence ever came to light. After news of the baby got out, the media descended on Karla once again. In April 2007, it was reported that Karla had a new husband, Thierry Bordelais.

Karla must not have been able to live with the media scrutiny because, in December 2007, newspapers and online news sites widely reported that she had fled Canada for the Caribbean and will be applying for citizenship in her new country.

~

Notes on Sources

Bagby, David. *Dance with the Devil: A Memoir of Murder and Loss*. Toronto: Key Porter Books, 2007.

Blatchford, Christie. "Coarse Villains, Shining Heroes: Trial begins for two women who stabbed officer to death." (Toronto ed.). *National Post*, October 15, 1999. p. A1.

Blatchford, Christie. "Living in a World of Neglect, Abuse, Breeds Hopelessness" and "Freedom: Another word for nothing left to lose" (all but Toronto edition). *National Post*, Oct 21, 1999. p. A9.

Dawson, Michelle. *The Murder of Charles-Antoine Blais*. http://www.sentex.net/~nexus23/naa_03.html. Accessed September 2007.

Markesteyn, Peter H., and David C. Quay, *Findings of Turner Review and Investigation*. St. John's: Government of Newfoundland and Labrador, 2006.

Priest, Lisa. *Women Who Killed*. Toronto: McClelland and Stewart, 1992.

Vallée, Brian. *Life With Billy*. Toronto: Seal Books, 1986.

Vallée, Brian. *The Torso Murder: The Untold Story of Evelyn Dick*. Toronto: Key Porter Books, 2001.

Wiebe, Rudy. *Stolen Life: Journey of a Cree Woman*. Toronto: Vintage Canada, 1998.

Williams, Stephen. *Invisible Darkness: The Horrifying Case of Paul Bernardo and Karla Homlka.* Toronto: McArthur & Company, 1999.

Williams, Stephen. *Karla: A Pact with the Devil.* Toronto: Cantos, 2003.

Zacharias, Yvonne. "Burden of Autism Too Much for Mother." *Ottawa Citizen.* November 8, 1996. p. F10.

Zacharias, Yvonne, and Lisa Fitterman. "Mother Pleads Guilty to Drowning Son." *Ottawa Citizen.* March 25, 1997. p. A4.

About the Author

Patricia MacQuarrie

Patricia MacQuarrie studied criminology at the University of Alberta and has volunteered with RCMP and police services across the province. She taught English in Japan with her husband for three years and gave birth to the first of two sons there before deciding to move back to Canada. Patricia is a member of the Alberta Writer's Guild and is the treasurer and secretary of the her hometown writer's group. Her work has been published in the *Globe and Mail* and CBC's *Alberta Anthology*.

Check out more True Crime from

QUAGMIRE PRESS

MISSING!
The Disappeared, Lost or Abducted in Canada
by Lisa Wojna

This book is a fascinating if disturbing collection of true stories about Canadians who disappeared without a trace. Even if they or their remains were found eventually, mysteries remain to this day as to what really happened:

- The families of Ontario's Lost Boys still wonder what became of them after the six took a late-night cruise on Lake Ontario

- Nicole Hoar, planning a surprise visit to her sister in Smithers, disappeared hitchhiking along BC's infamous Highway of Tears

- Sex-trade workers had been disappearing from Vancouver's downtown Eastside for 20 years before law enforcement began investigating Robert William Pickton

- Despite national and international publicity, no one has stepped forward to identify a young man dubbed Mr. Nobody after a brutal beating put him in a Toronto hospital

And more...

$18.95 • Softcover • 5.25" X 8.25" • 264 pages
ISBN 10: 978-0978340-90-6 • ISBN 13: 978-0978340-90-2

Available from your local bookseller
or by contacting the distributor
Lone Pine Publishing
1-800-661-9017
www.lonepinepublishing.com

Check out more True Crime from

QUAGMIRE
PRESS

WRONGFULLY CONVICTED
The Innocent in Canada
By Peter Boer

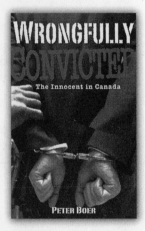

Their names have swept across this country like a wave since the 1990s—men and women in Canada who were convicted of murder, and after spending years and sometimes decades in prison, were later found innocent.

James Driskell, David Milgaard, Guy Paul Morin and Steven Truscott are the more well-known Canadians who have been wrongfully convicted of murder, but there are more dating back to the 1950s. Wilbert Coffin and Donald Marshall Jr. have also since been exonerated of murder convictions. However, Wilbert Coffin's innocence was discovered only after he was hanged.

In *Wrongfully Accused,* journalist Peter Boer tells the chilling stories of these men who were the subject of police incompetence, malicious prosecution and faulty testimony.

$18.95 • Softcover • 5.25" X 8.25" • 256 pages
ISBN 10: 978-0978340-91-4 • ISBN 13: 978-0978340-91-9

Available from your local bookseller
or by contacting the distributor
Lone Pine Publishing
1-800-661-9017
www.lonepinepublishing.com